SCENE IV
SCENE V
ACT THE THIRD
SCENE I
SCENE II
SCENE III
SCENE IV
SCENE V
SCENE VI
ACT THE FOURTH
SCENE I
SCENE II
SCENE III
SCENE IV
SCENE V
SCENE VI
SCENE VII
SCENE VIII
ACT THE FIFTH
SCENE I
SCENE II
SCENE III
SCENE IV
SCENE V
SCENE VII
SCENE VIII
SCENE IX
SCENE X
FOOTNOTES
HENRY THOMAS RILEY (TRANSLATOR)
TERENCE – A CONCISE BIBLIOGRAPHY

DRAMATIS PERSONÆ
LACHES,[1] an aged Athenian.

PHÆDRIA,[2] his son.
CHÆREA,[3] his son.
ANTIPHO,[4] a young man, friend of Chærea.
CHREMES,[5] a young man, brother of Pamphila.
THRASO,[6] a boastful Captain.
GNATHO,[7] a Parasite.
PARMENO,[8] servant of Phædria.
SANGA,[9] cook to Thraso.
DONAX,[10]
SIMALIO,[11] servants of Thraso.
SYRISCUS,[12]
DORUS,[15] a Eunuch slave.
THAIS [13] a Courtesan.
PYTHIAS,[14] her attendant.
DORIAS,[15] her attendant.
SOPHRONA,[16] a nurse.
PAMPHILA,[17] a female slave.

SCENE:—Athens; before the houses of Laches and Thais.

THE SUBJECT

A certain citizen of Athens had a daughter named Pamphila, and a son called Chremes. The former was stolen while an infant, and sold to a Rhodian merchant, who having made a present of her to a Courtesan of Rhodes, she brought her up with her own daughter Thais, who was somewhat older. In the course of years, Thais following her mother's way of life, removes to Athens. Her mother dying, her property is put up for sale, and Pamphila is purchased as a slave by Thraso, an officer and an admirer of Thais, who happens just then to be visiting Rhodes. During the absence of Thraso, Thais becomes acquainted with Phædria, an Athenian youth, the son of

Laches; she also discovers from Chremes, who lives near Athens, that Pamphila, her former companion, is his sister. Thraso returns, intending to present to her the girl he has bought, but determines not to do so until she has discarded Phædria. Finding that the girl is no other than Pamphila, Thais is at a loss what to do, as she both loves Phædria, and is extremely anxious to recover Pamphila. At length, to please the Captain, she excludes Phædria, but next day sends for him, and explains to him her reasons, at the same time begging of him to allow Thraso the sole right of admission to her house for the next two days, and assuring him that as soon as she shall have gained possession of the girl, she will entirely throw him off. Phædria consents, and resolves to spend these two days in the country; at the same time he orders Parmeno to take to Thais a Eunuch and an Æthiopian girl, whom he has purchased for her. The Captain also sends Pamphila, who is accidentally seen by Chærea, the younger brother of Phædria; he, being smitten with her beauty, prevails upon Parmeno to introduce him into the house of Thais, in the Eunuch's dress. Being admitted there, in the absence of Thais, he ravishes the damsel. Shortly afterward Thraso quarrels with Thais, and comes with all his attendants to her house to demand the return of Pamphila, but is disappointed. In conclusion, Pamphila is recognized by her brother Chremes, and is promised in marriage to Chremes; while Thraso becomes reconciled to Phædria, through the mediation of Gnatho, his Parasite.

THE TITLE OF THE PLAY [18]

Performed at the Megalensian Games; L. Posthumius Albinus and L. Cornelius Merula being Curule Ædiles. L. Ambivius Turpio and L. Atilius Præsnestinus performed it. Flaccus, the freedman of Claudius, composed the music to two treble flutes. From the Greek of Menander. It was acted twice,[19] M. Valerius and C. Fannius being Consuls.[20]

EUNUCHUS; THE EUNUCH

THE SUMMARY OF C. SULPITIUS APOLLINARIS

The Captain, Thraso, being ignorant of the same, has brought from abroad a girl who used wrongly to be called the sister of Thais, and presents her to Thais herself: she in reality is a citizen of Attica. To the same woman, Phædria, an admirer of Thais, orders a Eunuch whom he has purchased, to be taken, and he himself goes away into the country, having been entreated to give up two days to Thraso. A youth, the brother of Phædria, having fallen in love with the damsel sent to the house of Thais, is dressed up in the clothes of the Eunuch. Parmeno prompts him; he goes in; he ravishes the maiden; but at length her brother being discovered, a citizen of Attica, betroths her who has been ravished, to the youth, and Thraso prevails upon Phædria by his entreaties.

THE PROLOGUE

If there is any one who desires to please as many good men as possible, and to give offense to extremely few, among those does our Poet enroll his name. Next, if there is one who thinks[21] that language too harsh, is here applied to him, let him bear this in mind—that it is an answer, not an attack; inasmuch as he has himself been the first aggressor; who, by translating plays verbally,[22] and writing them in bad Latin, has made out of good Greek Plays Latin ones by no means good. Just as of late he has published the Phasma[23] [the Apparition] of Menander; and in the Thesaurus [the Treasure] has described[24] him from whom the gold is demanded, as pleading his cause why it should be deemed his own, before the person who demands it has stated how this treasure belongs to him, or how it came into the tomb of his father.

Henceforward, let him not deceive himself, or fancy thus, "I have now done with it; there's nothing that he can say to me." I recommend him not to be mistaken, and to refrain from provoking me. I have many other points, as to which for the present he shall be pardoned, which, however, shall be brought forward hereafter, if he persists in attacking me, as he has begun to do. After the Ædiles had purchased the Eunuch of Menander, the Play which we are about to perform, he managed to get an opportunity of viewing it.[25] When the magistrates were present it began to be performed. He exclaimed that a thief, no Poet, had produced the piece, but still had not deceived[26] him; that, in fact, it was the Colax, an old Play of Plautus;[27] and that from it were taken the characters of the Parasite and the Captain. If this is a fault, the fault is the ignorance of the Poet; not that he intended to be guilty of theft. That so it is, you will now be enabled to judge. The Colax is a Play of Menander's; in it there is Colax, a Parasite, and a braggart Captain: he does not deny that he has transferred these characters into his Eunuch from the Greek; but assuredly he does deny this, that he was aware that those pieces had been already translated into Latin. But if it is not permitted us to use the same characters as others, how can it any more be allowed to represent hurrying servants,[28] to describe virtuous matrons, artful courtesans, the gluttonous parasite, the braggart captain, the infant palmed off, the old man cajoled by the servant, about love, hatred, suspicion? In fine, nothing is said now that has not been said before. Wherefore it is but just that you should know this, and make allowance, if the moderns do what the ancients used to do. Grant me your attention, and give heed in silence, that you may understand what the Eunuch means.

ACT THE FIRST

SCENE I

Enter **PHÆDRIA** and **PARMENO**.

PHÆDRIA
What, then, shall I do?[29] Ought I not to go, not now even, when I am sent for of her own accord? Or ought I rather so to behave myself as not to put up with affronts from Courtesans? She shut her door against me; she now invites me back. Ought I to return? No; though she should implore me.

PARMENO
I'faith, if indeed you only can, there's nothing better or more spirited; but if you begin, and can not hold out stoutly, and if, when you can not endure it, while no one asks you, peace being not made, you come to her of your own accord, showing that you love her, and can not endure it, you are done for; it's all over with you; you are ruined outright. She'll be jilting you, when she finds you overcome. Do you then, while there's time, again and again reflect upon this, master, that a matter, which in itself admits of neither prudence nor moderation, you are unable to manage with prudence. In love there are all these evils; wrongs, suspicions, enmities, reconcilements, war, then peace; if you expect to render these things, naturally uncertain, certain by dint of reason, you wouldn't effect it a bit the more than if you were to use your endeavors to be mad with reason. And, what you are now, in anger, meditating to yourself, "What! I to her?[30] Who—him! Who—me! Who wouldn't? Only let me alone; I had rather die; she shall find out what sort of a person I am;" these expressions, upon my faith, by a single false tiny tear, which, by rubbing her eyes, poor thing, she can hardly squeeze out perforce, she will put an end to; and she'll be the first to accuse you; and you will be too ready to give satisfaction to her.

PHÆDRIA
O disgraceful conduct! I now perceive, both that she is perfidious, and that I am a wretched man. I am both weary of her, and burn

with passion; knowing and fully sensible, alive and seeing it, I am going to ruin; nor do I know what I am to do.

PARMENO
What you are to do? Why, only to redeem yourself, thus captivated, at the smallest price you can; if you can not at a very small rate, still for as little as you can; and do not afflict yourself.

PHÆDRIA
Do you persuade me to this?

PARMENO
If you are wise. And don't be adding to the troubles which love itself produces; those which it does produce, bear patiently. But see, here she is coming herself, the downfall of our fortunes,[31]—for that which we ought ourselves to enjoy she intercepts.

SCENE II

Enter **THAIS** from her house.

THAIS [To herself, not seeing them]
Ah wretched me! I fear lest Phædria should take it amiss or otherwise than I intended it, that he was not admitted yesterday.

PHÆDRIA [Aside to **PARMENO**]
I'm trembling and shivering all over, Parmeno, at the sight of her.

PARMENO [Apart]
Be of good heart; only approach this fire,[32] you'll soon be warmer than you need.

THAIS [Turning round]

Who is it that's speaking here? What, are you here, my Phædria? Why are you standing here! Why didn't you come into the house at once?

PARMENO [Whispering to **PHÆDRIA**]
But not a word about shutting you out!

THAIS
Why are you silent?

PHÆDRIA
Of course, it's because[33] this door is always open to me, or because I'm the highest in your favor?

THAIS
Pass those matters by.

PHÆDRIA
How pass them by? O Thais, Thais, I wish that I had equal affection with yourself, and that it were in like degree, that either this, might distress you in the same way that it distresses me, or that I might be indifferent at this being done by you.

THAIS
Prithee, don't torment yourself, my life, my Phædria. Upon my faith, I did it, not because I love or esteem any person more than you; but the case was such that it was necessary to be done.

PARMENO [Ironically]
I suppose that, poor thing, you shut him out of doors, for love, according to the usual practice.

THAIS
Is it thus you act, Parmeno? Well, well.
[To **PHÆDRIA**]

But listen—the reason for which I desired you to be sent for hither—

PHÆDRIA
Go on.

THAIS [Pointing to **PARMENO**]
First tell me this; can this fellow possibly hold his tongue?

PARMENO
What, I? Perfectly well. But, hark you, upon these conditions I pledge my word to you; the truth that I hear, I'm silent upon, and retain it most faithfully; but if I hear what's false and without foundation, it's out at once; I'm full of chinks, and leak in every direction. Therefore, if you wish it to be kept secret, speak the truth.

THAIS
My mother was a Samian; she lived at Rhodes—

PARMENO
That may be kept a secret.

THAIS
There, at that period, a certain merchant made present to my mother of a little girl, who had been stolen away from Attica here.

PARMENO
What, a citizen?

THAIS
I think so; we do not know for certain: she herself used to mention her mother's and her father's name; her country and other tokens she didn't know, nor, by reason of her age, was she able. The merchant added this: that he had heard from the kidnappers that she had been carried off from Sunium.[34] When my mother

received her, she began carefully to teach her every thing, and to bring her up, just as though she had been her own daughter. Most persons supposed that she was my sister. Thence I came hither with that stranger, with whom alone at that period I was connected; he left me all which I now possess—

PARMENO
Both these things are false; out it goes.

THAIS
How so?

PARMENO
Because you were neither content with one, nor was he the only one to make you presents; for he likewise—
[Pointing to **PHÆDRIA**]
—brought a pretty considerable share to you.

THAIS
Such is the fact; but do allow me to arrive at the point I wish. In the mean time, the Captain, who had begun to take a fancy to me, set out to Caria;[35] since when, in the interval, I became acquainted with you. You yourself are aware how very dear I have held you; and how I confess to you all my nearest counsels.

PHÆDRIA
Nor will Parmeno be silent about that.

PARMENO
O, is that a matter of doubt?

THAIS
Attend; I entreat you. My mother died there recently; her brother is somewhat greedy after wealth. When he saw that this damsel was of beauteous form and understood music, hoping for a good price, he forthwith put her up for sale, and sold her. By good fortune this

friend of mine was present; he bought her as a gift to me, not knowing or suspecting any thing of all this. He returned; but when he perceived that I had formed a connection with you as well, he feigned excuses on purpose that he might not give her; he said that if he could feel confidence that he should be preferred to yourself by me, so as not to apprehend that, when I had received her, I should forsake him, then he was ready to give her to me; but that he did fear this. But, so far as I can conjecture, he has set his affections upon the girl.

PHÆDRIA
Any thing beyond that?

THAIS
Nothing; for I have made inquiry. Now, my Phædria, there are many reasons why I could wish to get her away from him. In the first place, because she was called my sister; moreover, that I may restore and deliver her to her friends. I am a lone woman; I have no one here, neither acquaintance nor relative; wherefore, Phædria, I am desirous by my good offices to secure friends. Prithee, do aid me in this, in order that it may be the more easily effected. Do allow him for the few next days to have the preference with me. Do you make no answer?

PHÆDRIA
Most vile woman! Can I make you any answer after such behavior as this?

PARMENO
Well done, my master, I commend you;
[Aside]
—he's galled at last.
[To **PHÆDRIA**]
You show yourself a man.

PHÆDRIA

I was not aware what you were aiming at; "she was carried away from here, when a little child; my mother brought her up as though her own; she was called my sister; I wish to get her away, that I may restore her to her friends." The meaning is, that all these expressions, in fine, now amount to this, that I am shut out, he is admitted. For what reason? Except that you love him more than me: and now you are afraid of her who has been brought hither, lest she should win him, such as he is, from yourself.

THAIS
I, afraid of that?

PHÆDRIA
What else, then, gives you concern? Let me know. Is he the only person who makes presents? Have you found my bounty shut against you? Did I not, when you told me that you wished for a servant-maid from Æthiopia,[36] setting all other matters aside, go and seek for one? Then you said that you wanted a Eunuch, because ladies of quality[37] alone make use of them; I found you one. I yesterday paid twenty minæ[38] for them both. Though slighted by you, I still kept these things in mind; as a reward for so doing, I am despised by you.

THAIS
Phædria, what does this mean? Although I wish to get her away, and think that by these means it could most probably be effected; still, rather than make an enemy of you, I'll do as you request me.

PHÆDRIA
I only wish that you used that expression from your heart and truthfully, "rather than make an enemy of you." If I could believe that this was said sincerely, I could put up with any thing.

PARMENO [Aside]
He staggers; how instantaneously is he vanquished by a single expression!

THAIS
I, wretched woman, not speak from my heart? What, pray, did you ever ask of me in jest, but that you carried your point? I am unable to obtain even this of you, that you would grant me only two days.

PHÆDRIA
If, indeed, it is but two days; but don't let these days become twenty.

THAIS
Assuredly not more than two days, or—

PHÆDRIA
"Or?" I won't have it.

THAIS
It shall not be; only do allow me to obtain this of you.

PHÆDRIA
Of course that which you desire must be done.

THAIS
I love you as you deserve; you act obligingly.

PHÆDRIA [To **PARMENO**]
I shall go into the country; there I shall worry myself for the next two days: I'm resolved to do so; Thais must be humored. Do you, Parmeno, take care that they are brought hither.

PARMENO
Certainly.

PHÆDRIA
For the next two days then, Thais, adieu.

THAIS
And the same to you, my Phædria; do you desire aught else?

PHÆDRIA
What should I desire? That, present with the Captain, you may be as if absent; that night and day you may love me; may feel my absence; may dream of me; may be impatient for me; may think about me; may hope for me; may centre your delight in me; may be all in all with me; in fine, if you will, be my very life, as I am yours.

[Exeunt **PHÆDRIA** and **PARMENO**.

SCENE III

THAIS
alone.

THAIS [To herself]
Ah wretched me![39] perhaps now he puts but little faith in me, and forms his estimate of me from the dispositions of other women.[40] By my troth, I, who know my own self, am very sure of this, that I have not feigned any thing that's false, and that no person is dearer to my heart than this same Phædria; and whatever in the present case I have done, for this girl's sake have I done it; for I trust that now I have pretty nearly discovered her brother, a young man of very good family; and he has appointed this day to come to me at my house. I'll go hence in-doors, and wait until he comes.

[She goes into her house.

ACT THE SECOND

SCENE I

Enter **PHÆDRIA** and **PARMENO**.

PHÆDRIA
Mind that those people are taken there, as I ordered.

PARMENO
I'll do so.

PHÆDRIA
And carefully.

PARMENO
It shall be done.

PHÆDRIA
And with all speed.

PARMENO
It shall be done.

PHÆDRIA
Have you had sufficient instructions?

PARMENO
Dear me! to ask the question, as though it were a matter of difficulty. I wish that you were able, Phædria, to find any thing as easily as this present will be lost.

PHÆDRIA
Together with it, I myself am lost, which concerns me more nearly. Don't bear this with such a feeling of vexation.

PARMENO

By no means; on the contrary, I'll see it done. But do you order any thing else?

PHÆDRIA
Set off my present with words, as far as you can; and so far as you are able, do drive away that rival of mine from her.

PARMENO
Pshaw! I should have kept that in mind, even if you hadn't reminded me.

PHÆDRIA
I shall go into the country and remain there.

PARMENO
I agree with you.

[Moves as if going.

PHÆDRIA
But hark you!

PARMENO
What is it you want?

PHÆDRIA
Are you of opinion that I can muster resolution and hold out so as not to come back within the time?

PARMENO
What, you? Upon my faith, I don't think so; for either you'll be returning at once, or by-and-by, at night, want of sleep will be driving you hither.

PHÆDRIA

I'll do some laborious work, that I may be continually fatigued, so as to sleep in spite of myself.

PARMENO
When wearied, you will be keeping awake; by this you will be making it worse.

PHÆDRIA
Oh, you talk to no purpose, Parmeno: this softness of spirit, upon my faith, must be got rid of; I indulge myself too much. Could I not do without her, pray, if there were the necessity, even for a whole three days?

PARMENO
Whew! an entire three days! Take care what you are about.

PHÆDRIA
My mind is made up.

[Exit.

SCENE II

PARMENO alone.

PARMENO [To himself]
Good Gods! What a malady is this! That a man should become so changed through love, that you wouldn't know him to be the same person! Not any one was there[41] less inclined to folly than he, and no one more discreet or more temperate. But who is it that's coming this way? Heyday! surely this is Gnatho, the Captain's Parasite; he's bringing along with him the damsel as a present to her. Heavens! How beautiful! No wonder if I make but a sorry figure

here to-day with this decrepit Eunuch of mine. She surpasses Thais herself.

[Stands aside.

SCENE III

Enter **GNATHO** at a distance, leading **PAMPHILA**.

GNATHO [To himself]
Immortal Gods! how much does one man excel another! What a difference there is between a wise person and a fool! This strongly came into my mind from the following circumstance. As I was coming along to-day, I met a certain person of this place, of my own rank and station, no mean fellow, one who, like myself, had guttled away his paternal estate; I saw him, shabby, dirty, sickly, beset with rags and years;—"What's the meaning of this garb?" said I; he answered, "Because, wretch that I am, I've lost what I possessed: see to what I am reduced,—all my acquaintances and friends forsake me." On this I felt contempt for him in comparison with myself. "What!" said I, "you pitiful sluggard, have you so managed matters as to have no hope left? Have you lost your wits together with your estate? Don't you see me, who have risen from the same condition? What a complexion I have, how spruce and well dressed, what portliness of person? I have every thing, yet have nothing; and although I possess nothing, still, of nothing am I in want." "But I," said he, "unhappily, can neither be a butt nor submit to blows."[42] "What!" said I, "do you suppose it is managed by those means? You are quite mistaken. Once upon a time, in the early ages, there was a calling for that class; this is a new mode of coney-catching; I, in fact, have been the first to strike into this path. There is a class of men who strive to be the first in every thing, but are not; to these I make my court; I do not present myself to them to be laughed at; but I am the first to laugh with them, and at the same time to admire their

parts: whatever they say, I commend; if they contradict that self-same thing, I commend again. Does any one deny? I deny: does he affirm? I affirm: in fine, I have so trained myself as to humor them in every thing. This calling is now by far the most productive."

PARMENO [Apart]
A clever fellow, upon my faith! From being fools he makes men mad outright.

GNATHO [To himself, continuing]
While we were thus talking, in the mean time we arrived at the market-place; overjoyed, all the confectioners ran at once to meet me; fishmongers,[43] butchers, cooks,[44] sausage-makers, and fishermen, whom, both when my fortunes were flourishing and when they were ruined, I had served, and often serve still: they complimented me, asked me to dinner, and gave me a hearty welcome. When this poor hungry wretch saw that I was in such great esteem, and that I obtained a living so easily, then the fellow began to entreat me that I would allow him to learn this method of me; I bade him become my follower[45] if he could; as the disciples of the Philosophers take their names from the Philosophers themselves, so too, the Parasites ought to be called Gnathonics.

PARMENO [Apart to the **AUDIENCE**]
Do you see the effects of ease and feeding at another's cost?

GNATHO [To himself, continuing]
But why do I delay to take this girl to Thais, and ask her to come to dinner?
[Aside, on seeing **PARMENO**]
But I see Parmeno, our rival's servant, waiting before the door of Thais with a sorrowful air; all's safe; no doubt these people are finding a cold welcome. I'm resolved to have some sport with this knave.

PARMENO [Aside]

They fancy that, through this present, Thais is quite their own.

GNATHO [Accosting **PARMENO**]
With his very best wishes Gnatho greets Parmeno, his very good friend.—What are you doing?

PARMENO
I'm standing.[46]

GNATHO
So I perceive. Pray, do you see any thing here that don't please you?

PARMENO
Yourself.

GNATHO
I believe you,—but any thing else, pray?

PARMENO
Why so?

GNATHO
Because you are out of spirits.

PARMENO
Not in the least.

GNATHO [Pointing to her]
Well, don't be so; but what think you of this slave?

PARMENO
Really, not amiss.

GNATHO [Aside]
I've galled the fellow.

PARMENO [Aside, on overhearing him]
How mistaken you are in your notion!

GNATHO
How far do you suppose this gift will prove acceptable to Thais?

PARMENO
It's this you mean to say now, that we are discarded there. Hark you, there are vicissitudes in all things.

GNATHO
For the next six months, Parmeno, I'll set you at ease; you sha'n't have to be running to and fro, or sitting up till daylight. Don't I make you happy?

PARMENO
Me? O prodigiously!

GNATHO
That's my way with my friends.

PARMENO
I commend you.

GNATHO
I'm detaining you; perhaps you were about to go somewhere else.

PARMENO
Nowhere.

GNATHO
In that case then, lend me your services a little; let me be introduced to her.

PARMENO

Very well;
[**GNATHO** knocks at the door, which immediately opens]
—now the door is open for you—
[Aside]
—because you are bringing her.

GNATHO [Going into the house of **THAIS** ironically]
Should you like any one to be called out from here?

[Goes in with **PAMPHILA**, and shuts the door.

SCENE IV

PARMENO, alone.

PARMENO [To himself]
Only let the next two days go by; you who, at present, in such high favor, are opening the door with one little finger, assuredly I'll cause to be kicking at that door full oft, with your heels, to no purpose.

[Re-enter **GNATHO** from the house.

GNATHO
Still standing here, Parmeno? Why now, have you been left on guard here, that no go-between might perchance be secretly running from the Captain to her?

[Exit.

PARMENO
Smartly said; really they ought to be wonderful things to please the Captain. But I see my master's youngest son coming this way; I wonder why he has come away from the Piraeus,[47] for he is at present on guard there in the public service. It's not for nothing;

he's coming in a hurry, too; I can't imagine why he's looking around in all directions.

SCENE V

Enter **CHÆREA** on the other side of the stage, in haste.

CHÆREA [To himself]
I'm utterly undone! The girl is nowhere; nor do I know where I am myself, to have lost sight of her. Where to inquire for her, where to search for her, whom to ask, which way to turn, I'm at a loss. I have only this hope; wherever she is, she can not long be concealed. O what beauteous features! from this moment I banish all other women from my thoughts; I can not endure these every-day beauties.

PARMENO [Apart]
Why look, here's the other one. He's saying something, I don't know what, about love. O unfortunate old man, their father! This assuredly is a youth, who, if he does begin, you will say that the other one was mere play and pastime, compared with what the madness of this one will cause.

CHÆREA [To himself, aloud]
May all the Gods and Goddesses confound that old fellow who detained me to-day, and me as well who stopped for him, and in fact troubled myself a straw about him. But see, here's Parmeno. [Addressing him]
Good-morrow to you.

PARMENO
Why are you out of spirits, and why in such a hurry? Whence come you?

CHÆREA
What, I? I'faith, I neither know whence I'm come, nor whither I'm going; so utterly have I lost myself.

PARMENO
How, pray?

CHÆREA
I'm in love.

PARMENO [Starting]
Ha!

CHÆREA
Now, Parmeno, you may show what sort of a man you are. You know that you often promised me to this effect: "Chærea, do you only find some object to fall in love with; I'll make you sensible of my usefulness in such matters," when I used to be storing up my father's provisions for you on the sly in your little room.[48]

PARMENO
To the point, you simpleton.

CHÆREA
Upon my faith, this is the fact. Now, then, let your promises be made good, if you please, or if indeed the affair is a deserving one for you to exert your energies upon. The girl isn't like our girls, whom their mothers are anxious to have with shoulders kept down, and chests well girthed,[49] that they may be slender. If one is a little inclined to plumpness, they declare that she's training for a boxer,[50] and stint her food; although their constitutions are good, by their treatment they make them as slight as bulrushes; and so for that reason they are admired, forsooth.

PARMENO
What sort of a girl is this one of yours?

CHÆREA
A new style of beauty.

PARMENO [Ironically]
Astounding!

CHÆREA
Her complexion genuine,[51] her flesh firm and full of juiciness.[52]

PARMENO
Her age?

CHÆREA
Her age? Sixteen.

PARMENO
The very flower of youth.[53]

CHÆREA
Do you make it your care to obtain her for me either by force, stealth, or entreaty; so that I only gain her, it matters not how to me.

PARMENO
Well, but to whom does the damsel belong?

CHÆREA
That, i'faith, I don't know.

PARMENO
Whence did she come?

CHÆREA
That, just as much.

PARMENO
Where does she live?

CHÆREA
Nor yet do I know that.

PARMENO
Where did you see her?

CHÆREA
In the street.

PARMENO
How did you come to lose her?

CHÆREA
Why, that's what I was just now fretting myself about; and I do not believe that there is one individual to whom all good luck is a greater stranger than to myself. What ill fortune this is! I'm utterly undone!

PARMENO
What's the matter?

CHÆREA
Do you ask me? Do you know Archidemides, my father's kinsman and years'-mate?

PARMENO
Why not?

CHÆREA
He, while I was in full pursuit of her, met me.

PARMENO
Unseasonably, upon my faith.

CHÆREA
Aye, unhappily, rather; for other ordinary matters are to be called "unseasonable," Parmeno. It would be safe for me to make oath that I have not seen him for fully these six or seven months, until just now, when I least wanted, and there was the least occasion. Come now! isn't this like a fatality? What do you say?

PARMENO
Extremely so.

CHÆREA
At once he came running up to me, from a considerable distance, stooping, palsied, hanging his lip, and wheezing. "Halloo, Chærea! halloo!" said he; "I've something to say to you." I stopped. "Do you know what it is I want with you?" said he. "Say on," said I. "To-morrow my cause comes on," said he. "What then?" "Be sure and tell your father to remember and be my advocate[54] in the morning." In talking of this, an hour elapsed.[55] I inquired if he wanted any thing else. "That's all," said he. I left him. When I looked in this direction for the damsel, she had that very instant turned thia way down this street of ours.

PARMENO [Aside]
It's a wonder if he doesn't mean her who has just now been made a present of to Thais here.

CHÆREA
When I got here, she was nowhere to be seen.

PARMENO
Some attendants, I suppose, were accompanying the girl?

CHÆREA
Yes; a Parasite, and a female servant.

PARMENO [Apart]
It's the very same.
[To **CHÆREA**]
It's all over with you; make an end of it; you've said your last.[56]

CHÆREA
You are thinking about something else.

PARMENO
Indeed I'm thinking of this same matter.

CHÆREA
Pray, tell me, do you know her, or did you see her?

PARMENO
I did see, and I do know her; I am aware to what house she has been taken.

CHÆREA
What, my dear Parmeno, do you know her, and are you aware where she is?

PARMENO
She has been brought here—
[Pointing]
—to the house of Thais the Courtesan.[57] She has been made a present to her.

CHÆREA
What opulent person is it, to be presenting a gift so precious as this?

PARMENO
The Captain Thraso, Phædria's rival.

CHÆREA

An unpleasant business for my brother, it should seem.

PARMENO
Aye, and if you did but know what present he is pitting against this present, you would say so still more.

CHÆREA
Troth now, what is it, pray?

PARMENO
A Eunuch.[58]

CHÆREA
What! that unsightly creature, pray, that he purchased yesterday, an old woman?

PARMENO
That very same.

CHÆREA
To a certainty, the gentleman will be bundled out of doors, together with his present; but I wasn't aware that this Thais is our neighbor.

PARMENO
It isn't long since she came.

CHÆREA
Unhappy wretch that I am! never to have seen her, even. Come now, just tell me, is she as handsome as she is reported to be?[59]

PARMENO
Quite.

CHÆREA
But nothing in comparison with this damsel of mine?

PARMENO
Another thing altogether.

CHÆREA
Troth now, Parmeno, prithee do contrive for me to gain possession of her.

PARMENO
I'll do my best, and use all my endeavors; I'll lend you my assistance.

[Going.

Do you want any thing else with me?

CHÆREA
Where are you going now?

PARMENO
Home; to take those slaves to Thais, as your brother ordered me.

CHÆREA
Oh, lucky Eunuch that! really, to be sent as a present to that house!

PARMENO
Why so?

CHÆREA
Do you ask? Ho will always see at home a fellow-servant of consummate beauty, and he conversing with her; he will be in the same house with her; sometimes he will take his meals with her; sometimes sleep near her.

PARMENO
What now, if you yourself were to be this fortunate person?

CHÆREA
By what means, Parmeno? Tell me.

PARMENO
Do you assume his dress.

CHÆREA
His dress! Well, what then?

PARMENO
I'll take you there instead of him.

CHÆREA [Musing]
I hear you.

PARMENO
I'll say that you are he.

CHÆREA
I understand you.

PARMENO
You may enjoy those advantages which you just now said he would enjoy; you may take your meals together with her, be in company with her, touch her, dally with her, and sleep by her side; as not one of these women is acquainted with you, nor yet knows who you are. Besides, you are of an age and figure that you may easily pass for a eunuch.

CHÆREA
You speak to the purpose; I never knew better counsel given. Well, let's go in at once; dress me up, take me away, lead me to her, as fast as you can.

PARMENO
What do you mean? Really, I was only joking.

CHÆREA
You talk nonsense.

PARMENO
I'm undone! Wretch that I am! what have I done?
[**CHÆREA** pushes him along]
Whither are you pushing me? You'll throw me down presently. I entreat you, be quiet.

CHÆREA
Let's be off.

[Pushes him.

PARMENO
Do you still persist?

CHÆREA
I am resolved upon it.

PARMENO
Only take care that this isn't too rash a project.

CHÆREA
Certainly it isn't; let me alone for that.

PARMENO
Aye, but I shall have to pay the penalty[60] for this?

CHÆREA
Pshaw!

PARMENO
We shall be guilty of a disgraceful action.

CHÆREA
What, is it disgraceful[61] to be taken to the house of a Courtesan, and to return the compliment upon those tormentors who treat us and our youthful age so scornfully, and who are always tormenting us in every way;—to dupe them just as we are duped by them? Or is it right and proper that in preference my father should be wheedled out of his money by deceitful pretexts? Those who knew of this would blame me; while all would think the other a meritorious act.

PARMENO
What's to be done in such case? If you are determined to do it, you must do it: but don't you by-and-by be throwing the blame upon me.

CHÆREA
I shall not do so.

PARMENO
Do you order me, then?

CHÆREA
I order, charge, and command you; I will never disavow my authorizing you.

PARMENO
Follow me; may the Gods prosper it!

[They go into the house of **LACHES**.

ACT THE THIRD

SCENE I

Enter **THRASO** and **GNATHO**.

THRASO
Did Thais really return me many thanks?

GNATHO
Exceeding thanks.

THRASO
Was she delighted, say you?

GNATHO
Not so much, indeed, at the present itself, as because it was given by you; really, in right earnest, she does exult at that.

[Enter **PARMENO** unseen, from **LACHES'** house.

PARMENO [Apart]
I've come here to be on the look-out, that when there is an opportunity I may take the presents. But see, here's the Captain.

THRASO
Undoubtedly it is the case with me, that every thing I do is a cause for thankfulness.

GNATHO
Upon my faith, I've observed it.

THRASO
The most mighty King,[62] even, always used to give me especial thanks for whatever I did; but not so to others.

GNATHO
He who has the wit that you have, often by his words appropriates to himself the glory that has been achieved by the labor of others.

THRASO
You've just hit it.[63]

GNATHO
The king, then, kept you in his eye.[64]

THRASO
Just so.

GNATHO
To enjoy your society.

THRASO
True; he intrusted to me all his army, all his state secrets.

GNATHO
Astonishing!

THRASO
Then if, on any occasion, a surfeit of society, or a dislike of business, came upon him, when he was desirous to take some recreation; just as though—you understand?[65]

GNATHO
I know; just as though on occasion he would rid his mind of those anxieties.

THRASO
You have it. Then he used to take me aside as his only boon companion.

GNATHO
Whew! You are telling of a King of refined taste.

THRASO

Aye, he is a person of that sort; a man of but very few acquaintanceships.

GNATHO [Aside]
Indeed, of none,[66] I fancy, if he's on intimate terms with you.

THRASO
All the people envied me, and attacked me privately. I don't care one straw. They envied me dreadfully; but one in particular, whom the King had appointed over the Indian elephants.[67] Once, when he became particularly troublesome, "Prithee, Strato," said I, "are you so fierce because you hold command over the wild beasts?"

GNATHO
Cleverly said, upon my faith, and shrewdly. Astounding! You did give the fellow a home thrust. What said he?

THRASO
Dumfounded, instantaneously.

GNATHO
How could he be otherwise?

PARMENO [Apart]
Ye Gods, by our trust in you! a lost and miserable fellow the one, and the other a scoundrel.

THRASO
Well then, about that matter, Gnatho, the way in which I touched up the Rhodian at a banquet—did I never tell you?

GNATHO
Never; but pray, do tell me.
[Aside]
I've heard it more than a thousand times already.

THRASO
There was in my company at a banquet, this young man of Rhodes, whom I'm speaking of. By chance I had a mistress there; he began to toy with her, and to annoy me. "What are you doing, sir impudence?" said I to the fellow; "a hare yourself, and looking out for game?"[68]

GNATHO [Pretending to laugh very heartily]
Ha, ha, ha!

THRASO
What's the matter?

GNATHO
How apt, how smart, how clever; nothing could be more excellent. Prithee, was this a saying of yours? I fancied it was an old one.

THRASO
Did you ever hear it before?

GNATHO
Many a time; and it is mentioned among the first-rate ones.

THRASO
It's my own.

GNATHO
I'm sorry though that it was said to a thoughtless young man, and one of respectability.

PARMENO [Apart]
May the Gods confound you!

GNATHO
Pray, what did he do?

THRASO
Quite disconcerted. All who were present were dying with laughter; in short, they were all quite afraid of me.

GNATHO
Not without reason.

THRASO
But hark you, had I best clear myself of this to Thais, as to her suspicion that I'm fond of this girl?

GNATHO
By no means: on the contrary, rather increase her jealousy.

THRASO
Why so?

GNATHO
Do you ask me? Don't you see, if on any occasion she makes mention of Phædria or commends him, to provoke you—

THRASO
I understand.

GNATHO
That such may not be the case, this method is the only remedy. When she speaks of Phædria, do you instantly mention Pamphila. If at any time she says, "Let's invite Phædria to make one," do you say, "Let's ask Pamphila to sing." If she praises his good looks, do you, on the other hand, praise hers. In short, do you return like for like, which will mortify her.

THRASO
If, indeed, she loved me,[69] this might be of some use, Gnatho.

GNATHO

Since she is impatient for and loves that which you give her, she already loves you; as it is, then, it is an easy matter for her to feel vexed. She will be always afraid lest the presents which she herself is now getting, you may on some occasion be taking elsewhere.

THRASO
Well said; that never came into my mind.

GNATHO
Nonsense. You never thought about it; else how much more readily would you yourself have hit upon it, Thraso!

SCENE II

Enter **THAIS** from her house, attended by **PYTHIAS**.

THAIS [As she comes out]
I thought I just now heard the Captain's voice. And look, here he is. Welcome, my dear Thraso.

THRASO
O my Thais, my sweet one, how are you? How much do you love me in return for that music girl?

PARMENO [Apart]
How polite! What a beginning he has made on meeting her!

THAIS
Very much, as you deserve.

GNATHO
Let's go to dinner then.
[To **THRASO**]
What do you stand here for?

PARMENO [Apart]
Then there's the other one: you would declare that he was born for his belly's sake.

THRASO
When you please; I sha'n't delay.

PARMENO [Apart]
I'll accost them, and pretend as though I had just come out.

[He comes forward.

Are you going any where, Thais?

THAIS
Ha! Parmeno; well done; just going out for the day.

PARMENO
Where?

THAIS [Aside, pointing at **THRASO**]
Why! don't you see him?

PARMENO [Aside]
I see him, and I'm sorry for it.
[Aloud]
Phædria's presents are ready for you when you please.

THRASO [Impatiently]
Why are we to stand here? Why don't we be off?

PARMENO [To **THRASO**]
Troth now, pray, do let us, with your leave, present to her the things we intend, and accost and speak to her.

THRASO [Ironically]
Very fine presents, I suppose, or at least equal to mine.

PARMENO
The fact will prove itself.
[Goes to the door of **LACHES'** house and calls]
Ho there! bid those people come out of doors at once, as I ordered.

[Enter from the house a **BLACK GIRL**.

PARMENO
Do you step forward this way,—
[To **THAIS**]
She comes all the way from Æthiopia.

THRASO [Contemptuously]
Here are some three minæ in value.

GNATHO
Hardly so much.

PARMENO
Where are you, Dorus? Step this way.

[Enter **CHÆREA** from the house, dressed like the **EUNUCH**.

PARMENO
There's a Eunuch for you—of what a genteel appearance! of what a prime age!

THAIS
God bless me, he's handsome.

PARMENO
What say you, Gnatho? Do you see any thing to find fault with? And what say you, Thraso?

[Aside]
They hold their tongues; they praise him sufficiently thereby.
[To **THAIS**]
Make trial of him in literature, try him in exercises,[70] and in music; I'll warrant him well skilled in what it becomes a gentleman to know.

THRASO
That Eunuch, if occasion served,[71] even in my sober senses, I—

PARMENO
And he who has sent these things makes no request that you will live for him alone, and that for his own sake others may be excluded; he neither tells of battles nor shows his scars, nor does he restrict you as
[Looking at **THRASO**]
—a certain person does; but when it is not inconvenient, whenever you think fit, whenever you have the time, he is satisfied to be admitted.

THRASO [To **GNATHO**, contemptuously]
It appears that this is the servant of some beggarly, wretched master.

GNATHO
Why, faith, no person, I'm quite sure of that, could possibly put up with him, who had the means to get another.

PARMENO
You hold your tongue—a fellow whom I consider beneath all men of the very lowest grade: for when you can bring yourself to flatter that fellow
[Pointing at **THRASO**]
I do believe you could pick your victuals out of the very flames.[72]

THRASO

Are we to go now?

THAIS
I'll take these in-doors first
[Pointing to **CHÆREA** and the **ÆTHIOPIAN**]
—and at the same time I'll order what I wish; after that I'll return immediately.

[Goes into the house with **PYTHIAS**, **CHÆREA**, and the **SLAVE**.

THRASO [To **GNATHO**]
I shall be off. Do you wait for her.

PARMENO
It is not a proper thing for a general to be walking in the street with a mistress.

THRASO
Why should I use many words with you? You are the very ape of your master.

[Exit **PARMENO**.

GNATHO [Laughing]
Ha, ha, ha!

THRASO
What are you laughing at?

GNATHO
At what you were mentioning just now; that saying, too, about the Rhodian, recurred to my mind. But Thais is coming out.

THRASO
You go before; take care that every thing is ready at home.

GNATHO
Very well.

[Exit.

[Re-enter **THAIS** with **PYTHIAS** and **FEMALE ATTENDANTS**.

THAIS
Take care, Pythias, and be sure that if Chremes should happen to come,[73] to beg him to wait; if that is not convenient, then to come again; if he can not do that, bring him to me.

PYTHIAS
I'll do so.

THAIS
Well, what else was I intending to say? O, do you take particular care of that young woman; be sure that you keep at home.

THRASO
Let us begone.

THAIS [To her **ATTENDANTS**]
You follow me.

[Exeunt **THAIS** and **THRASO**, followed by the Attendants. **PYTHIAS** goes into the house.

SCENE III

Enter **CHREMES**.

CHREMES [To himself]

Why, really, the more and more I think of it, I shouldn't be surprised if this Thais should be doing me some great mischief; so cunningly do I perceive myself beset by her. Even on the occasion when she first requested me to be fetched to her (any one might ask me, "What business had you with her?" Really I don't know.) When I came, she found an excuse for me to remain there; she said that she had been offering a sacrifice,[74] and that she was desirous to speak upon some important business with me. Even then I had a suspicion that all these things were being done for her artful purposes. She takes her place beside me; pays every attention to me; seeks an opportunity of conversation. When the conversation flagged, she turned off to this point—how long since my father and mother died? I said that it was now a long time ago. Whether I had any country-house at Sunium, and how far from the sea? I suppose that this has taken her fancy, and she expects to get it away from me. Then at last, whether any little sister of mine had been lost from there; whether any person was with her; what she had about her when she was lost; whether any one could recognize her. Why should she make these inquiries? Unless, perhaps, she pretends— so great is her assurance—that she herself is the same person that was formerly lost when a little girl. But if she is alive, she is sixteen years old, not older; whereas Thais is somewhat older than I am. She has sent to press me earnestly to come. Either let her speak out what she wants, or not be troublesome; I assuredly shall not come a third time—

[Knocking at the door of **THAIS**]

Ho! there, ho! there! Is any one here? It's I, Chremes.

SCENE IV

Enter **PYTHIAS** from the house.

PYTHIAS
O most charming, dear creature!

CHREMES [Apart]
I said there was a design upon me.

PYTHIAS
Thais entreated you most earnestly to come again to-morrow.

CHREMES
I'm going into the country.

PYTHIAS
Do, there's a dear sir.

CHREMES
I can not, I tell you.

PYTHIAS
Then stay here at our house till she comes back.

CHREMES
Nothing less likely.

PYTHIAS
Why, my dear Chremes?

[Taking hold of him.

CHREMES [Shaking her off]
Away to perdition with you!

PYTHIAS
If you are so determined about it, pray do step over to the place where she is.

CHREMES
I'll go there.

PYTHIAS [Calling at the door]
Here, Dorias
[**DORIAS** enters]
—show this person directly to the Captain's.

[Exit **CHREMES** with **DORIAS**, **PYTHIAS** goes into the house.

SCENE V

Enter **ANTIPHO**.

ANTIPHO [To himself]
Yesterday some young fellows of us agreed together at the Piræus that we were to go shares today in a club-entertainment. We gave Chærea charge of this matter; our rings were given[75] as pledges; the place and time arranged. The time has now gone by; at the place appointed there was nothing ready. The fellow himself is nowhere to be met with; I neither know what to say nor what to suppose. Now the rest have commissioned me with this business, to look for him. I'll go see, therefore, if he's at home. But who's this, I wonder, coming out of Thais's? Is it he, or is it not? 'Tis the very man! What, sort of being is this? What kind of garb is this? What mischief is going on now? I can not sufficiently wonder or conjecture. But, whatever it is, I should like first at a distance to try and find out.

[He stands apart.

SCENE VI

Enter **CHÆREA** from the house of Thais, in the Eunuch's dress.

CHÆREA [Looking around, then aloud to himself]
Is there anybody here? There's no one. Is there any one following me from there? There's not a person. Now am I not at liberty to give vent to these raptures? O supreme Jupiter! now assuredly is the time for me to meet my death,[76] when I can so well endure it; lest my life should sully this ecstasy with some disaster. But is there now no inquisitive person to be intruding upon me, to be following me wherever I go, to be deafening me, worrying me to death, with asking questions; why thus transported, or why so overjoyed, whither I'm going, whence I'm come, where I got this garb, what is my object, whether I'm in my senses or whether downright mad?

ANTIPHO [Apart]
I'll accost him, and I'll do him the favor which I see he's wishing for.
[Accosting him]
Chærea, why are you thus transported? What's the object of this garb? Why is it that you're so overjoyed? What is the meaning of this? Are you quite right in your senses? Why do you stare at me? What have you to say?

CHÆREA
O joyous day! O welcome, my friend! There's not one in all the world whom I would rather wish to see at this moment than yourself.

ANTIPHO
Pray, do tell me what all this means.

CHÆREA
Nay rather, i'faith, I beg of you to listen to me. Do you know the mistress whom my brother is so fond of?

ANTIPHO
I know her; I suppose you mean Thais?

CHÆREA
The very same.

ANTIPHO
So far I recollect.

CHÆREA
To-day a certain damsel was presented to her. Why now should I extol or commend her beauty to you, Antipho, since you yourself know how nice a judge of beauty I am? I have been smitten by her.

ANTIPHO
Do you say so?

CHÆREA
If you saw her, I am sure you would say she's exquisite. What need of many words? I fell in love with her. By good luck there was at our house a certain Eunuch, whom my brother had purchased for Thais, and he had not as yet been sent to her. On this occasion, Parmeno, our servant, made a suggestion to me, which I adopted.

ANTIPHO
What was it?

CHÆREA
Be quiet, and you shall hear the sooner; to change clothes with him, and order myself to be taken there in his stead.

ANTIPHO
What, instead of the Eunuch?

CHÆREA
The fact.

ANTIPHO
To receive what advantage, pray, from this plan?

CHÆREA
Do you ask? That I might see, hear, and be in company with her whom I loved, Antipho. Is that a slight motive, or a poor reason? I was presented to the woman. She, as soon as she received me, joyfully took me home to her house and intrusted the damsel—

ANTIPHO
To whom? To you?

CHÆREA
To me.

ANTIPHO [Ironically]
In perfect safety, at all events.

CHÆREA
She gave orders that we male was to come near her, and commanded me not to stir away from her; that I was to remain alone with her in the inner apartments.[77] Looking bashfully on the ground, I nodded assent.

ANTIPHO [Ironically]
Poor fellow!

CHÆREA [Continuing]
"I am going out," said she, "to dinner." She took her maids with her; a few novices of girls[78] remained, to be about her. These immediately made preparations for her to bathe. I urged them to make haste. While preparations were being made, the damsel sat in a room looking up at a certain painting,[79] in which was represented how Jove[80] is said once to have sent a golden shower into the bosom of Danaë. I myself began to look at it as well, and as he had in former times played the like game, I felt extremely delighted that a God should change himself into money, and slily come through the tiles of another person's house, to deceive the

fair one by means of a shower. But what God was this? He who shakes the most lofty temples of heaven with his thunders. Was I, a poor creature of a mortal,[81] not to do the same? Certainly, I was to do it, and without hesitation. While I was thinking over these matters with myself, the damsel meantime was fetched away to bathe; she went, bathed, and came back; after which they laid her on a couch. I stood waiting to see if they gave me any orders. One came up, "Here, Dorus," said she, "take this fan,[82] and let her have a little air in this fashion, while we are bathing; when we have bathed, if you like, you may bathe too." With a demure air I took it.

ANTIPHO
Really, I should very much have liked to see that impudent face of yours just then, and what figure a great donkey like you made, holding a fan!

CHÆREA [Continuing]
Hardly had she said this, when all, in a moment, betook themselves off: away they went to bathe, and chattered aloud;[83] just as the way is when masters are absent. Meanwhile, sleep overtook the damsel; I slyly looked askance[84] through the fan;[85] this way—
[Showing how]
—at the same time I looked round in all directions, to see whether all was quite safe. I saw that it was. I bolted the door.

ANTIPHO
What then?

CHÆREA
Eh? What then, you simpleton?

ANTIPHO
I own I am.

CHÆREA

Was I to let slip the opportunity offered me, so excellent, so short-lived,[86] so longed for, so unexpected. In that case, i'faith, I really should have been the person I was pretending to be.

ANTIPHO
Troth, you certainly are in the right; but, meantime, what has been arranged about the club-entertainment?

CHÆREA
All's ready.

ANTIPHO
You are a clever band; but where? At your house?

CHÆREA
No, at Discus's, our freedman.

ANTIPHO
That's a long way off.

CHÆREA
Then let's make so much the greater haste.

ANTIPHO
Change your dress.

CHÆREA
Where am I to change it? I'm at a loss; for at present I'm an exile from home; I'm afraid of my brother, lest he should be in-doors: and then again of my father, lest he should have returned from the country by this.

ANTIPHO
Let's go to my house; there is the nearest place for you to change.

CHÆREA

You say right. Let's be off; besides, I want to take counsel with you about this girl, by what means I may be able to secure the future possession of her.

ANTIPHO
Very well.

[Exeunt.

ACT THE FOURTH

SCENE I

Enter **DORIAS**, with a casket in her hand.

DORIAS [To herself]
So may the Gods bless me, but from what I have seen, I'm terribly afraid that this mad fellow will be guilty of some disturbance to-day or of some violence to Thais. For when this young man, the brother of the damsel, arrived, she begged the Captain to order him to be admitted; he immediately began to get into a passion, and yet didn't dare refuse; Thais still insisted that he would invite the man in. This she did for the sake of detaining him; because there was no opportunity just then of telling him what she wanted to disclose about her sister. He was invited in, and took his seat. Then she entered into discourse with him. But the Captain, fancying it was a rival brought before his very eyes, wanted in his turn to mortify her: "Hark you, boy," said he, "go fetch Pamphila, that she may amuse us here." She exclaimed, "At a banquet! Certainly not." The Captain still persisted to a downright quarrel. Meanwhile my mistress secretly took off her golden jewels,[87] and gave them to me to take away: this is a sign, I'm sure, that she'll betake herself from there as soon as she possibly can.

[Goes into the house.

SCENE II

Enter **PHÆDRIA**.

PHÆDRIA [To himself]
While I was going[88] into the country, I began on the road, as it mostly happens when there is any anxiety on the mind, to reflect with myself upon one thing after another, and upon every thing in the worst light. What need of words? While I was musing thus, inadvertently I passed my country-house. I had already got some distance from it, when I perceived this; I returned again, really feeling quite uneasy; when I came to the very turning that leads to the house, I came to a stop, and began to reason with myself; "What! must I stay here alone for two days without her? Well, and what then? It's nothing at all. What? Nothing at all? Well now, if I haven't the privilege of touching her, am I not even to have that of seeing her? If I may not do the one, at least I may the other. Surely to love at a distance[89] even, is better than nothing at all." I purposely passed the house. But how's this, that Pythias is suddenly hurrying out in such a fright?

[Stands apart.

SCENE III

Enter **PYTHIAS** and **DORIAS** in haste from the house of **THAIS**.

PYTHIAS [Aloud]

Where, wretch that I am, shall I find this wicked and impious fellow? Or where look for him? That he should dare to commit so audacious a crime as this! I'm ruined outright!

PHÆDRIA [Apart]
I dread what this may be.

PYTHIAS
Besides, too, the villain, after he had abused the girl, rent all the poor thing's clothes, and tore her hair as well.

PHÆDRIA [Apart, in surprise]
Ha!

PYTHIAS
If he were just now in my reach, how eagerly would I fly at that villain's eyes with my nails!

PHÆDRIA [Apart]
Really I can't imagine what disturbance has happened to us at home in my absence. I'll accost them.
[Going up to them]
What's the matter? Why in such haste? Or whom are you looking for, Pythias?

PYTHIAS
Why, Phædria, whom should I be looking for? Away with you, as you deserve, with such fine presents of yours.

PHÆDRIA
What is the matter?

PYTHIAS
What, do you ask? The Eunuch you gave us, what confusion he has caused. He has ravished the girl whom the Captain made present of to my mistress.

PHÆDRIA
What is it you say?

PYTHIAS
I'm ruined outright!

PHÆDRIA
You are drunk.

PYTHIAS
I wish that they were so, who wish ill to me.

DORIAS
Oh, prithee, my dear Pythias, what a monstrous thing this is!

PHÆDRIA
You are out of your senses. How could a Eunuch possibly do this?

PYTHIAS
I know nothing about him: as to what he has done, the thing speaks for itself. The girl is in tears; and when you ask her what's the matter, she does not dare tell. But he, a precious fellow, is nowhere to be seen. To my sorrow I suspect too, that when he took himself off he carried something away from the house.

PHÆDRIA
I can not enough wonder, whither this varlet can possibly have betaken himself to any distance from here; unless perhaps he has returned home to our house.

PYTHIAS
Pray, go and see whether he is there.

PHÆDRIA
I'll let you know immediately.

[Goes into the house of **LACHES**.

DORIAS
Ruined outright! Prithee, my dear, I never did so much as hear of a deed so abominable!

PYTHIAS
Why, faith, I had heard that they were extremely fond of the women, but were incapable; unfortunately what has happened never came into my mind; otherwise I should have shut him up somewhere, and not have intrusted the girl to him.

SCENE IV

Enter **PHÆDRIA** from the house of **LACHES**, with **DORUS** in **CHÆREA'S** clothes.

PHÆDRIA [Dragging him out]
Come out, you villain! What, do you lag behind, you runaway? Out with you, you sorry bargain!

DORUS [Crying out]
Mercy, I do entreat you!

PHÆDRIA
Oh, do look at that! How the villain distorts his face. What means your coming back hither? Why this change of dress? What have you to say? If I had delayed a moment, Pythias, I shouldn't have found him at home: he had just prepared, in this fashion, for flight.

[Pointing at his dress.

PYTHIAS

Have you caught the fellow, pray?

PHÆDRIA
Caught him, why not?

PYTHIAS
O well done!

DORIAS
Upon my faith that really is capital!

PYTHIAS
Where is he?

PHÆDRIA
Do you ask the question? Don't you see him?

[Pointing to the **EUNUCH**.

PYTHIAS [Staring about]
See whom, pray?

PHÆDRIA
This fellow, to be sure

[Pointing.

PYTHIAS
What person is this?

PHÆDRIA
The same that was brought to your house to-day.

PYTHIAS
Not one of our people has ever beheld this person with her eyes, Phædria.

PHÆDRIA
Not beheld him?

PYTHIAS
Prithee, did you fancy that this was he who was brought to our house?

PHÆDRIA
Why, I had no other.

PYTHIAS
O dear! this one really isn't to be compared with the other. He was of a handsome and genteel appearance.

PHÆDRIA
He seemed so, just then, because he was decked out in party-colored clothes:[90] now he appears ugly, for this reason—because he hasn't got them on.

PYTHIAS
Prithee, do hold your tongue; as though indeed the difference was so trifling. A young man was brought to our house to-day, whom, really, Phædria, you would have liked to look upon. This is a withered, antiquated, lethargic, old fellow, with a speckled complexion.[91]

PHÆDRIA [Starting]
Hah! What tale is this? You'll so be-fool me that I sha'n't know what I bought.
[To **DORUS**]
How now, sirrah, did I not buy you?

DORUS
You did buy me.

PYTHIAS
Bid him answer me in my turn.

PHÆDRIA
Question him.

PYTHIAS [To **DORUS**]
Did you come here to-day to our house?
[**DORUS** shakes his head]
He says, no. But it was the other one that came, about sixteen years of age; whom Parmeno brought with him.

PHÆDRIA [To **DORUS**]
Well now, in the first place tell me this, where did you get that dress that you have on? What, are you silent? Monster of a fellow, are you not going to speak.

[Shakes him.

DORUS
Chærea came.

PHÆDRIA
What, my brother?

DORUS
Yes.

PHÆDRIA
When?

DORUS
To-day.

PHÆDRIA
How long since?

DORUS
Just now.

PHÆDRIA
With whom?

DORUS
With Parmeno.

PHÆDRIA
Did you know him before?

DORUS
No.

PHÆDRIA
How did you know he was my brother?

DORUS
Parmeno said he was. He gave me these clothes.

PHÆDRIA
I'm undone!

DORUS
He himself put on mine; afterward, they both went out together.

PYTHIAS
Now are you quite satisfied that I am sober, and that we have told you no falsehood? Is it now sufficiently evident that the girl has been ravished?

PHÆDRIA
Avaunt, you beast, do you believe what he says?

PYTHIAS
What is there to believe? The thing speaks for itself.

PHÆDRIA [Apart to **DORUS**]
Step aside a little this way. Do you hear?
[**DORUS** steps aside]
A little further still. That will do. Now tell me this once more; did Chærea take your clothes off you?

DORUS
He did.

PHÆDRIA
And did he put them on?

DORUS
He did.

PHÆDRIA
And was he brought here instead of you?

DORUS
Yes.

PHÆDRIA
Great Jupiter! O wicked and audacious fellow!

PYTHIAS
Woe unto me! Now at last will you believe that we have been insulted in a disgraceful manner?

PHÆDRIA
It is no wonder that you believe what the fellow says.
[Aside]
What I'm to do I know not.
[Aside to **DORUS**]

Hark you, deny it all again.
[Aloud]
Can I not this day extract the truth from you? Did you really see my brother Chærea?

DORUS
No.

PHÆDRIA
He can't be brought to confess without being punished, I see: follow me this way. At one moment he affirms, at another denies.
[Aside]
Ask pardon of me.

DORUS
Indeed, I do entreat you, Phædria.

PHÆDRIA [Kicking him]
Be off in-doors.

DORUS
Oh! oh!

PHÆDRIA [Aside]
How in any other fashion to get decently out of this I don't know; for really it's all up with me.
[Aloud, with pretended indignation]
Will you be trifling with me even here, you knave?

[Follows **DORUS** into the house.

SCENE V

PYTHIAS and **DORIAS**.

PYTHIAS

I'm as certain that this is the contrivance of Parmeno as that I'm alive.

DORIAS

So it is, no doubt.

PYTHIAS

I'faith, I'll find out a method to-day to be even with him. But now, what do you think ought to be done, Dorias?

DORIAS

Do you mean with regard to this girl?

PYTHIAS

Yes; whether I ought to mention it or be silent?

DORIAS

Upon my word, if you are prudent, you won't know what you do know, either about the Eunuch or the girl's misfortune. By this method you'll both rid yourself of all perplexity, and have done a service to her.[92] Say this only, that Dorus has run away.

PYTHIAS

I'll do so.

DORIAS

But don't I see Chremes? Thais will be here just now.

PYTHIAS

Why so?

DORIAS

Because when I came away from there, a quarrel had just commenced between them.

PYTHIAS
Take in these golden trinkets; I shall learn from him what's the matter.

[**DORIAS** takes the casket into the house.

SCENE VI

Enter **CHREMES**, somewhat drunk.

CHREMES
Heyday! upon my faith, I've been bamboozled: the wine that I've drunk has got the upper hand. But, so long as I was reclining, how extremely sober I did seem to myself to be; when I got up, neither feet nor senses were quite equal to their duty.

PYTHIAS
Chremes!

CHREMES [Turning round]
Who's that? What, Pythias; dear me, how much more charming you now seem to me than a short time since!

PYTHIAS
Troth now, you are much more merry, that's certain.

CHREMES
Upon my faith, it is a true saying, that "Venus grows cold without Ceres and Bacchus." But has Thais got here long before me?

PYTHIAS
Has she already come away from the Captain's?

CHREMES
A long time ago; an age since. There has been a most violent quarrel between them.

PYTHIAS
Did she say nothing about you following her?

CHREMES
Nothing at all; only, on going away, she gave me a nod.

PYTHIAS
Well now, wasn't that enough?

CHREMES
Why, I didn't know that she meant that, until the Captain gave me an explanation, because I was dull of comprehension; for he bundled me out of the house. But look, here she is; I wonder how it was I got here before her.

SCENE VII

Enter **THAIS**.

THAIS [To herself]
I really do believe that he'll be here presently, to force her away from me. Let him come; but if he touches her with a single finger, that instant his eyes shall be torn out. I can put up with his impertinences and his high-sounding words, as long as they remain words: but if they are turned into realities, he shall get a drubbing.

CHREMES
Thais, I've been here some time.

THAIS

O my dear Chremes, you are the very person I was wanting. Are you aware that this quarrel took place on your account, and that the whole of this affair, in fact, bore reference to yourself?

CHREMES
To me? How so, pray?

THAIS
Because, while I've been doing my best to recover and restore your sister to you, this and a great deal more like it I've had to put up with.

CHREMES
Where is she?

THAIS
At home, at my house.

CHREMES [Starting]
Hah!

THAIS
What's the matter? She has been brought up in a manner worthy of yourself and of her.

CHREMES
What is it you say?

THAIS
That which is the fact. Her I present to you, nor do I ask of you any return for her.

CHREMES
Thanks are both felt and shall be returned in such way, Thais, as you deserve.

THAIS
But still, take care, Chremes, that you don't lose her, before you receive her from me; for it is she, whom the Captain is now coming to take away from me by force. Do you go, Pythias, and bring out of the house the casket with the tokens.[93]

CHREMES [Looking down the side Scene]
Don't you see him, Thais?

PYTHIAS [To **THAIS**]
Where is it put?

THAIS
In the clothes' chest. Tiresome creature, why do you delay?

[**PYTHIAS** goes into the house.

CHREMES
What a large body of troops the Captain is bringing with him against you. Bless me!

THAIS
Prithee, are you frightened, my dear sir?

CHREMES
Get out with you. What, I frightened? There's not a man alive less so.

THAIS
Then now is the time to prove it.

CHREMES
Why, I wonder what sort of a man you take me to be.

THAIS

Nay, and consider this too; the person that you have to deal with is a foreigner;[94] of less influence than you, less known, and one that has fewer friends here.

CHREMES
I'm aware of that; but it's foolish to run the risk of what you are able to avoid. I had rather we should prevent it, than, having received an injury, avenge ourselves upon him. Do you go in and fasten the door, while I run across hence to the Forum; I should like us to have the aid of some legal adviser in this disturbance.

[Moves, as if going.

THAIS [Holding him]
Stay.

CHREMES
Let me go, I'll be here presently.

THAIS
There's no occasion, Chremes. Only say that she is your sister, and that you lost her when a little girl, and have now recognized her; then show the tokens.

[Re-enter **PYTHIAS** from the house, with the trinkets.

PYTHIAS [Giving them to **THAIS**]
Here they are.

THAIS [Giving them to **CHREMES**]
Take them. If he offers any violence, summon the fellow to justice; do you understand me?

CHREMES
Perfectly.

THAIS
Take care and say this with presence of mind.

CHREMES
I'll take care.

THAIS
Gather up your cloak.
[Aside]
Undone! the very person whom I've provided as a champion, wants one himself.

[They all go into the house.]

SCENE VIII

Enter **THRASO**, followed by **GNATHO**, **SANGA**, and other **ATTENDANTS**.

THRASO
Am I to submit, Gnatho, to such a glaring affront as this being put upon me? I'd die sooner. Simalio, Donax, Syriscus, follow me! First, I'll storm the house.

GNATHO
Quite right.

THRASO
I'll carry off the girl.

GNATHO
Very good.

THRASO

I'll give her own self a mauling.

GNATHO
Very proper.

THRASO [Arranging the **MEN**]
Advance hither to the main body, Donax, with your crowbar; you, Simalio, to the left wing; you, Syriscus, to the right. Bring up the rest; where's the centurion Sanga, and his maniple[95] of rogues?

SANGA [Coming forward]
See, here he is.

THRASO
What, you booby, do you think of fighting with a dish-clout,[96] to be bringing that here?

SANGA
What, I? I knew the valor of the general, and the prowess of the soldiers; and that this could not possibly go on without bloodshed; how was I to wipe the wounds?

THRASO
Where are the others?

SANGA
Plague on you, what others? Sannio is the only one left on guard at home.

THRASO [To **GNATHO**]
Do you draw up your men in battle order; I'll be behind the second rank;[97] from that position I'll give the word to all.

[Takes his place behind the second rank.

GNATHO [Aside]

That's showing prudence; as soon as he has drawn them up, he secures a retreat for himself.

THRASO [Pointing to the arrangements]
This is just the way Pyrrhus used to proceed.[98]

[**CHREMES** and **THAIS** appear above at a window.

CHREMES
Do you see, Thais, what plan he is upon? Assuredly, that advice of mine about closing the door was good.

THAIS
He who now seems to you to be a hero, is in reality a mere vaporer; don't be alarmed.

THRASO [To **GNATHO**]
What seems best to you?

GNATHO
I could very much[99] like a sling to be given you just now, that you might pelt them from here on the sly at a distance; they would be taking to flight.

THRASO [To **GNATHO**]
But look—
[Pointing]
I see Thais there herself.

GNATHO
How soon are we to fall to?

THRASO
Hold—
[Holding him back]

—it behooves a prudent person to make trial of every thing before arms. How do you know but that she may do what I bid her without compulsion?

GNATHO
Ye Gods, by our trust in you, what a thing it is to be wise! I never come near you but what I go away from you the wiser.

THRASO
Thais, in the first place, answer me this. When I presented you that girl, did you not say that you would give yourself up to me alone for some days to come?

THAIS
Well, what then?

THRASO
Do you ask the question? You, who have been and brought your lover under my very eyes? What business had you with him? With him, too, you clandestinely betook yourself away from me.

THAIS
I chose to do so.

THRASO
Then give me back Pamphila; unless you had rather she were taken away by force.

CHREMES
Give her back to you, or you lay hands upon her? Of all the—

GNATHO
Ha! What are you about? Hold your tongue.

THRASO
What do you mean? Am I not to touch my own?

CHREMES
Your own, indeed, you gallows-bird![100]

GNATHO [To **CHREMES**]
Have a care, if you please. You don't know what kind of man you are abusing now.

CHREMES [To **GNATHO**]
Won't you be off from here? Do you know how matters stand with you? If you cause any disturbance here to-day, I'll make you remember the place, and day, and me too, for the rest of your life.

GNATHO
I pity you, who are making so great a man as this your enemy.

CHREMES
I'll break your head this instant if you are not off.

GNATHO
Do you really say so, puppy? Is it that you are at?

THRASO [To **CHREMES**]
What fellow are you? What do you mean? What business have you with her?

CHREMES
I'll let you know: in the first place, I assert that she is a freeborn woman.

THRASO [Starting]
Ha!

CHREMES
A citizen of Attica.

THRASO
Whew!

CHREMES
My own sister.

THRASO
Brazen face!

CHREMES
Now, therefore, Captain, I give you warning; don't you use any violence toward her. Thais, I'm going to Sophrona, the nurse, that I may bring her here and show her these tokens.

THRASO
What! Are you to prevent me from touching what's my own?

CHREMES
I will prevent it, I tell you.

GNATHO [To **THRASO**]
Do you hear him? He is convicting himself of theft. Is not that enough for you?

THRASO
Do you say the same, Thais?

THAIS
Go, find some one to answer you.

[She and **CHREMES** go away from the window.

THRASO [To **GNATHO**]
What are we to do now?

GNATHO

Why, go back again: she'll soon be with you, of her own accord, to entreat forgiveness.

THRASO
Do you think so?

GNATHO
Certainly, yes. I know the disposition of women: when you will, they won't; when you won't, they set their hearts upon you of their own inclination.

THRASO
You judge right.

GNATHO
Shall I dismiss the army then?

THRASO
Whenever you like.

GNATHO
Sanga, as befits gallant soldiers,[101] take care in your turn to remember your homes and hearths.

SANGA
My thoughts have been for some time among the sauce-pans.

GNATHO
You are a worthy fellow.

THRASO [Putting himself at their head]
You follow me this way.

[Exeunt **OMNES**.

ACT THE FIFTH

SCENE I

Enter **THAIS** from her house, followed by **PYTHIAS**.

THAIS
What! do you persist, hussy, in talking ambiguously to me? "I do know;" "I don't know;" "he has gone off;" "I have heard;" "I wasn't there." Don't you mean to tell me plainly, whatever it is? The girl in tears, with her garments torn, is mute; the Eunuch is off: for what reason? What has happened? Won't you speak?

PYTHIAS
Wretch that I am, what am I to say to you? They declare that he was not a Eunuch.

THAIS
What was he then?

PYTHIAS
That Chærea.

THAIS
What Chærea?

PYTHIAS
That stripling, the brother of Phædria.

THAIS
What's that you say, you hag?

PYTHIAS
And I am satisfied of it.

THAIS
Pray, what business had he at my house? What brought him there?

PYTHIAS
I don't know; unless, as I suppose, he was in love with Pamphila.

THAIS
Alas! to my confusion, unhappy woman that I am, I'm undone, if what you tell me is true. Is it about this that the girl is crying?

PYTHIAS
I believe so.

THAIS
How say you, you arch-jade? Did I not warn you about this very thing, when I was going away from here?

PYTHIAS
What could I do? Just as you ordered, she was intrusted to his care only.

THAIS
Hussy, I've been intrusting the sheep to the wolf. I'm quite ashamed to have been imposed upon in this way. What sort of man was he?

PYTHIAS
Hush! hush! mistress, pray; we are all right. Here we have the very man.

THAIS
Where is he?

PYTHIAS
Why there, to the left. Don't you see?

THAIS

I see.

PYTHIAS
Order him to be seized as quickly as possible.

THAIS
What can we do to him, simpleton?

PYTHIAS
What do to him, do you ask? Pray, do look at him; if his face doesn't seem an impudent one.

THAIS
Not at all.

PYTHIAS
Besides, what effrontery he has.

SCENE II

Enter **CHÆREA**, in the Eunuch's dress, on the other side of the stage.

CHÆREA [To himself]
At Antipho's,[102] both of them, father and mother, just as if on purpose, were at home, so that I couldn't any way get in, but that they must have seen me. In the mean time, while I was standing before the door, a certain acquaintance of mine was coming full upon me. When I espied him, I took to my heels as fast as I could down a narrow unfrequented alley; thence again to another, and thence to another; thus have I been most dreadfully harassed with running about, that no one might recognize me. But isn't this Thais that I see? It is she. I'm at a stand. What shall I do? But what need I care? What can she do to me?

THAIS [To **PYTHIAS**]
Let's accost him.
[To **CHÆREA**]
Good Mister Dorus, welcome; tell me, have you been running away?

CHÆREA
Madam, I did so.

THAIS
Are you quite pleased with it?

CHÆREA
No.

THAIS
Do you fancy that you'll get off with impunity?

CHÆREA
Forgive this one fault; if I'm ever guilty of another, then kill me.

THAIS
Were you in fear of my severity?

CHÆREA
No.

THAIS
No? What then?

CHÆREA [Pointing at **PYTHIAS**]
I was afraid of her, lest she might be accusing me to you.

THAIS
What had you done?

CHÆREA
A mere trifle.

PYTHIAS
Come now, a trifle, you impudent fellow. Does this appear a trifle to you, to ravish a virgin, a citizen?

CHÆREA
I took her for my fellow-servant.

PYTHIAS
Fellow-servant? I can hardly restrain myself from flying at his hair. A miscreant! Even of his own free will he comes to make fun of us.

THAIS [To **PYTHIAS**]
Won't you begone from here, you mad woman?

PYTHIAS
Why so? Really, I do believe I should be something in this hang-dog's debt, if I were to do so; especially as he owns that he is your servant.

THAIS
We'll pass that by. Chærea, you have behaved unworthily of yourself; for if I am deserving in the highest degree of this affront, still it is unbecoming of you to be guilty of it. And, upon my faith, I do not know what method now to adopt about this girl: you have so confounded all my plans, that I can not possibly return her to her friends in such a manner as is befitting and as I had intended; in order that, by this means, I might, Chærea, do a real service to myself.

CHÆREA
But now, from henceforth, I hope, Thais, that there will be lasting good-will between us. Many a time, from some affair of this kind

and from a bad beginning, great friendships have sprung up. What if some Divinity has willed this?

THAIS
I'faith, for my own part I both take it in that view and wish to do so.

CHÆREA
Yes, prithee, do so. Be sure of this one thing, that I did not do it for the sake of affronting you, but in consequence of passion.

THAIS
I understand, and, i'faith, for that reason do I now the more readily forgive you. I am not, Chærea, of a disposition so ungentle, or so inexperienced, as not to know what is the power of love.

CHÆREA
So may the Deities kindly bless me, Thais; I am now smitten with you as well.

PYTHIAS
Then, i'faith, mistress, I foresee you must have a care of him.

CHÆREA
I would not dare—

PYTHIAS
I won't trust you at all in any thing.

THAIS [To **PYTHIAS**]
Do have done.

CHÆREA
Now I entreat you that you will be my assistant in this affair. I intrust and commit myself to your care; I take you, Thais, as my protectress; I implore you; I shall die if I don't have her for my wife.

THAIS
But if your father should say any thing—

CHÆREA
Oh, he'll consent, I'm quite sure of that, if she is only a citizen.

THAIS
If you will wait a little, the brother himself of the young woman will be here presently; he has gone to fetch the nurse, who brought her up when a little child; you yourself, shall be present Chærea, at his recognition of her.

CHÆREA
I certainly will stay.

THAIS
In the mean time, until he comes, would you prefer that we should wait for him in the house, rather than here before the door?

CHÆREA
Why yes, I should like it much.

PYTHIAS [To **THAIS**]
Prithee, what are you going to do?

THAIS
Why, what's the matter?

PYTHIAS
Do you ask? Do you think of admitting him after this into your house?

THAIS
Why not?

PYTHIAS

Trust my word for it, he'll be creating some new disturbance.

THAIS
O dear, prithee, do hold your tongue.

PYTHIAS
You seem to me to be far from sensible of his assurance.

CHÆREA
I'll not do any thing, Pythias.

PYTHIAS
Upon my faith, I don't believe you, Chærea, except in case you are not trusted.

CHÆREA
Nay but, Pythias, do you be my keeper.

PYTHIAS
Upon my faith, I would neither venture to give any thing to you to keep, nor to keep you myself: away with you!

THAIS
Most opportunely the brother himself is coming.

CHÆREA
I'faith, I'm undone. Prithee, let's be gone in-doors, Thais. I don't want him to see me in the street with this dress on.

THAIS
For what reason, pray? Because you are ashamed?

CHÆREA
Just so.

PYTHIAS

Just so? But the young woman—

THAIS
Go first; I'll follow. You stay here, Pythias, that you may show Chremes in.

[**THAIS** and **CHÆREA** go into the house.

SCENE III

Enter **CHREMES** and **SOPHRONA**.

PYTHIAS [To herself]
Well! what now can suggest itself to my mind? What, I wonder, in order that I may repay the favor to that villain who palmed this fellow off upon us?

CHREMES
Really, do bestir yourself more quickly, nurse.

SOPHRONA
I am bestirring.

CHREMES
So I see; but you don't stir forward.

PYTHIAS [To **CHREMES**]
Have you yet shown the tokens to the nurse?

CHREMES
All of them.

PYTHIAS
Prithee, what does she say? Does she recognize them?

CHREMES
Yes, with a full recollection of them.

PYTHIAS
Upon my faith, you do bring good news; for I really wish well to this young woman. Go in-doors: my mistress has been for some time expecting you at home.

[**CHREMES** and **SOPHRONA** go into **THAIS'S** house.

But look, yonder I espy that worthy fellow, Parmeno, coming: just see, for heaven's sake, how leisurely he moves along. I hope I have it in my power to torment him after my own fashion. I'll go in-doors, that I may know for certain about the discovery; afterward I'll come out, and give this villain a terrible fright.

[Goes into the house.

SCENE IV

Enter **PARMENO**.

PARMENO [To himself]
I've just come back to see what Chærea has been doing here. If he has managed the affair with dexterity, ye Gods, by our trust in you, how great and genuine applause will Parmeno obtain! For not to mention that a passion, full of difficulty and expense, with which he was smitten for a virgin, belonging to an extortionate courtesan, I've found means of satisfying for him, without molestation, without outlay, and without cost; then, this other point—that is really a thing that I consider my crowning merit, to have found out the way by which a young man may be enabled to learn the

dispositions and manners of courtesans, so that by knowing them betimes, he may detest them ever after.

[**PYTHIAS** enters from the house unperceived.

For while they are out of doors, nothing seems more cleanly, nothing more neat or more elegant; and when they dine with a gallant, they pick daintily about:[103] to see the filth, the dirtiness, the neediness of these women; how sluttish they are when at home, and how greedy after victuals; in what a fashion they devour the black bread with yesterday's broth:—to know all this, is salvation to a young man.

SCENE V

Enter **PYTHIAS** from the house.

PYTHIAS [Apart, unseen by **PARMENO**]
Upon my faith, you villain, I'll take vengeance upon you for these sayings and doings; so that you sha'n't make sport of us with impunity.
[Aloud, coming forward]
O, by our trust in the Gods, what a disgraceful action! O hapless young man! O wicked Parmeno, to have brought him here!

PARMENO
What's the matter?

PYTHIAS
I do pity him; and so that I mightn't see it, wretched creature that I am, I hurried away out of doors. What a dreadful example they talk of making him!

PARMENO

O Jupiter! What is this tumult? Am I then undone? I'll accost her. What's all this, Pythias? What are you saying? An example made of whom?

PYTHIAS
Do you ask the question, you most audacious fellow? You've proved the ruin of the young man whom you brought hither for the Eunuch, while you were trying to put a trick upon us.

PARMENO
How so, or what has happened? Tell me.

PYTHIAS
I'll tell you: that young woman who was to-day made a present to Thais, are you aware that she is a citizen of this place, and that her brother is a person of very high rank?

PARMENO
I didn't know that.

PYTHIAS
But so she has been discovered to be; he, unfortunate youth, has ravished her. When the brother came to know of this being done, in a most towering rage, he—

PARMENO
Did what, pray?

PYTHIAS
First, bound him in a shocking manner.

PARMENO
Bound him?

PYTHIAS
And even though Thais entreated him that he wouldn't do so—

PARMENO
What is it you tell me?

PYTHIAS
Now he is threatening that he will also do that which is usually done to ravishers; a thing that I never saw done, nor wish to.

PARMENO
With what assurance does he dare perpetrate a crime so heinous?

PYTHIAS
How "so heinous?"

PARMENO
Is it not most heinous? Who ever saw any one taken up as a ravisher in a courtesan's house?

PYTHIAS
I don't know.

PARMENO
But that you mayn't be ignorant of this, Pythias, I tell you, and give you notice that he is my master's son.

PYTHIAS
How! Prithee, is it he?

PARMENO
Don't let Thais suffer any violence to be done to him. But why don't I go in myself?

PYTHIAS
Take care, Parmeno, what you are about, lest you both do him no good and come to harm yourself; for it is their notion, that whatever has happened, has originated in you.

PARMENO
What then, wretch that I am, shall I do, or how resolve? But look, I see the old gentleman returning from the country; shall I tell him or shall I not? By my troth, I will tell him; although I am certain that a heavy punishment is in readiness for me; but it's a matter of necessity, in order that he may rescue him.

PYTHIAS
You are wise. I'm going in-doors; do you relate to him every thing exactly as it happened.

[Goes into the house.

SCENE VI

Enter **LACHES**.

LACHES [To himself]
I have this advantage[104] from my country-house being so near at hand; no weariness, either of country or of town, ever takes possession of me; when satiety begins to come on, I change my locality. But is not that our Parmeno? Surely it is he. Whom are you waiting for, Parmeno, before the door here?

PARMENO [Pretends not to see him]
Who is it?
[Turning round]
Oh, I'm glad that you have returned safe.

LACHES
Whom are you waiting for?

PARMENO [Aside]

I'm undone: my tongue cleaves to my mouth through fright.

LACHES
Why, what is it you are trembling about? Is all quite right? Tell me.

PARMENO
Master, in the first place, I would have you persuaded of what is the fact; whatever has happened in this affair has happened through no fault of mine.

LACHES
What is it?

PARMENO
Really you have reason to ask. I ought first to have told you the circumstances. Phædria purchased a certain Eunuch, to make a present of to this woman here.

LACHES
To what woman?

PARMENO
To Thais.

LACHES
Bought? Good heavens, I'm undone! For how much?

PARMENO
Twenty minæ.

LACHES
Done for, quite.

PARMENO
Then, Chærea is in love with a certain music-girl here.

[Pointing to **THAIS'S** house.

LACHES
How! What? In love? Does he know already what a courtesan means? Is he come to town? One misfortune close upon another.

PARMENO
Master, don't look so at me; he didn't do these things by my encouragement.

LACHES
Leave off talking about yourself. If I live, you hang-dog, I'll— But first give me an account of it, whatever it is.

PARMENO
He was taken to the house of Thais in place of the Eunuch.

LACHES
In place of the Eunuch?

PARMENO
Such is the fact. They have since apprehended him in the house as a ravisher, and bound him.

LACHES
Death!

PARMENO
Mark the assurance of courtesans.

LACHES
Is there any other calamity or misfortune besides, that you have not told me of?

PARMENO
That's all.

LACHES
Do I delay rushing in here?

[Runs into the house of **THAIS**.

PARMENO [To himself]
There's no doubt but that I shall have a heavy punishment for this affair, only that I was obliged to act thus. I'm glad of this, that some mischief will befall these women here through my agency, for the old man has, for a long time, been on the look-out for some occasion[105] to do them a bad turn; at last he has found it.

SCENE VII

Enter **PYTHIAS** from the house of **THAIS** laughing.

PYTHIAS [To herself, on entering]
Never, upon my faith, for a long time past, has any thing happened to me that I could have better liked to happen, than the old gentleman just now, full of his mistake, coming into our house. I had the joke all to myself, as I knew[106] what it was he feared.

PARMENO [Apart]
Why, what's all this?

PYTHIAS
Now I'm come out to meet with Parmeno. But, prithee, where is he?

[Looking around.

PARMENO [Apart]
She's looking for me.

PYTHIAS
And there he is, I see; I'll go up to him.

PARMENO
What's the matter, simpleton? What do you mean? What are you laughing about? Still going on?

PYTHIAS [Laughing]
I'm dying; I'm wretchedly tired with laughing at you.

PARMENO
Why so?

PYTHIAS
Do you ask? Upon my faith, I never did see, nor shall see, a more silly fellow. Oh dear, I can not well express what amusement you've afforded in-doors. And still I formerly took you to be a clever and shrewd person. Why, was there any need for you instantly to believe what I told you? Or were you not content with the crime, which by your advice the young man had been guilty of, without betraying the poor fellow to his father as well? Why, what do you suppose his feelings must have been at the moment when his father saw him clothed in that dress? Well, do you now understand that you are done for?

PARMENO
Hah! what is it you say, you hussy? Have you been telling me lies? What, laughing still? Does it appear so delightful to you, you jade, to be making fools of us?

PYTHIAS [Laughing]
Very much so.

PARMENO
Yes, indeed, if you can do it with impunity.

PYTHIAS
Exactly so.

PARMENO
By heavens, I'll repay you!

PYTHIAS
I believe you; but, perhaps, that which you are threatening, Parmeno, will need a future day; you'll be trussed up directly, for rendering a silly young man remarkable for disgraceful conduct, and then betraying him to his father; they'll both be making an example of you.

[Laughing.

PARMENO
I'm done for!

PYTHIAS
This reward has been found you in return for that present of yours;[107] I'm off.

[Goes into the house.

PARMENO [To himself]
Wretch that I am; just like a rat, this day I've come to destruction through betrayal of myself.[108]

SCENE VIII

Enter **THRASO** and **GNATHO**.

GNATHO [To **THRASO**]

Well now? With what hope, or what design, are we come hither? What do you intend to do, Thraso?

THRASO
What, I? To surrender myself to Thais, and do what she bids me.

GNATHO
What is it you say?

THRASO
Why any the less so, than Hercules served Omphale.[109]

GNATHO
The precedent pleases me.
[Aside]
I only wish I may see your head stroked down with a slipper;[110] but her door makes a noise.

THRASO
Confusion! Why, what mischief's this? I never saw this person before; why, I wonder, is he rushing out in such a hurry?

[They stand aside.

SCENE IX

Enter **CHÆREA** from the house of **THAIS** on the other side of the stage.

CHÆREA [To himself, aloud]
O fellow-townsmen, is there any one alive more fortunate than me this day? Not any one, upon my faith: for clearly in me have the Gods manifested all their power, on whom, thus suddenly, so many blessings are bestowed.

PARMENO [Apart]
Why is he thus overjoyed?

CHÆREA [Seeing **PARMENO**, and running up to him]
O my dear Parmeno, the contriver, the beginner, the perfecter of all my delights, do you know what are my transports? Are you aware that my Pamphila has been discovered to be a citizen?

PARMENO
I have heard so.

CHÆREA
Do you know that she is betrothed to me?

PARMENO
So may the Gods bless me, happily done.

GNATHO [Apart to **THRASO**]
Do you hear what he says?

CHÆREA
And then, besides, I am delighted that my brother's mistress is secured to him; the family is united. Thais has committed herself to the patronage of my father;[111] she has put herself under our care and protection.

PARMENO
Thais, then, is wholly your brother's.

CHÆREA
Of course.

PARMENO
Then this is another reason for us to rejoice, that the Captain will be beaten out of doors.

CHÆREA
Wherever my brother is, do you take care that he hears this as soon as possible.

PARMENO
I'll go look for him at home.

[Goes into the house of **LACHES**.

THRASO [Apart to **GNATHO**]
Do you at all doubt, Gnatho, but that I am now ruined everlastingly?

GNATHO [To **THRASO**]
Without doubt, I do think so.

CHÆREA [To himself]
What am I to make mention of first, or commend in especial? Him who gave me the advice to do so, or myself, who ventured to undertake it? Or ought I to extol fortune, who has been my guide, and has so opportunely crowded into a single day events so numerous, so important; or my father's kindness and indulgence? Oh Jupiter, I entreat you, do preserve these blessings unto us!

SCENE X

Enter **PHÆDRIA** from the house of **LACHES**.

PHÆDRIA [To himself]
Ye Gods, by our trust in you, what incredible things has Parmeno just related to me! But where is my brother?

CHÆREA [Stepping forward]
Here he is.

PHÆDRIA
I'm overjoyed.

CHÆREA
I quite believe you. There is no one, brother, more worthy to be loved than this Thais of yours: so much is she a benefactress to all our family.

PHÆDRIA
Whew! are you commending her too to me?

THRASO [Apart]
I'm undone; the less the hope I have, the more I am in love. Prithee, Gnatho, my hope is in you.

GNATHO [Apart]
What do you wish me to do?

THRASO [Apart]
Bring this about, by entreaties or with money, that I may at least share Thais's favors in some degree.

GNATHO [Apart]
It's a hard task.

THRASO [Apart]
If you set your mind on any thing, I know you well. If you manage this, ask me for any present you like as your reward; you shall have what you ask.

GNATHO [Apart]
Is it so?

THRASO [Apart]
It shall be so.

GNATHO [Apart]
If I manage this, I ask that your house, whether you are present or absent, may be open to me; that, without invitation, there may always be a place for me.

THRASO [Apart]
I pledge my honor that it shall be so.

GNATHO [Apart]
I'll set about it then.

PHÆDRIA
Who is it I hear so close at hand?
[Turning round]
O Thraso—

THRASO [Coming forward]
Save you both—

PHÆDRIA
Perhaps you are not aware what has taken place here.

THRASO
I am quite aware.

PHÆDRIA
Why, then, do I see you in this neighborhood?

THRASO
Depending on your kindness.

PHÆDRIA
Do you know what sort of dependence you have? Captain, I give you notice, if ever I catch you in this street again, even if you should

say to me, "I was looking for another person, I was on my road this way," you are undone.

GNATHO
Come, come, that's not handsome.

PHÆDRIA
I've said it.

GNATHO
I didn't know you gave yourself such airs.

PHÆDRIA
So it shall be.

GNATHO
First hear a few words from me; and when I have said the thing, if you approve of it, do it.

PHÆDRIA
Let's hear.

GNATHO
Do you step a little that way, Thraso.
[**THRASO** stands aside]
In the first place, I wish you both implicitly to believe me in this, that whatever I do in this matter, I do it entirely for my own sake; but if the same thing is of advantage to yourselves, it would be folly for you not to do it.

PHÆDRIA
What is it?

GNATHO
I'm of opinion that the Captain, your rival, should be received among you.

PHÆDRIA [Starting]
Hah!

CHÆREA
Be received?

GNATHO [To **PHÆDRIA**]
Only consider. I'faith, Phaedria, at the free rate you are living with her, and indeed very freely you are living, you have but little to give; and it's necessary for Thais to receive a good deal. That all this may be supplied for your amour and not at your own expense, there is not an individual better suited or more fitted for your purpose than the Captain. In the first place, he both has got enough to give, and no one does give more profusely. He is a fool, a dolt, a blockhead; night and day he snores away; and you need not fear that the lady will fall in love with him; you may easily have him discarded whenever you please.

CHÆREA [To **PHÆDRIA**]
What shall we do?

GNATHO
And this besides, which I deem to be of even greater importance,—not a single person entertains in better style or more bountifully.

CHÆREA
It's a wonder if this sort of man can not be made use of in some way or other.

PHÆDRIA
I think so too.

GNATHO

You act properly. One thing I have still to beg of you,—that you'll receive me into your fraternity; I've been rolling that stone[112] for a considerable time past.

PHÆDRIA
We admit you.

CHÆREA
And with all my heart.

GNATHO
Then I, in return for this, Phaedria, and you, Chaerea, make him over to you[113] to be eaten and drunk to the dregs.

CHÆREA
Agreed.

PHÆDRIA
He quite deserves it.[114]

GNATHO [Calling to **THRASO**]
Thraso, whenever you please, step this way.

THRASO
Prithee, how goes it?

GNATHO
How? Why, these people didn't know you; after I had discovered to them your qualities, and had praised you as your actions and your virtues deserved, I prevailed upon them.

THRASO
You have managed well; I give you my best thanks. Besides, I never was any where but what all were extremely fond of me.

GNATHO [To **PHÆDRIA** and **CHÆREA**]

Didn't I tell you that he was a master of the Attic elegance?

PHÆDRIA
He is no other than you mentioned.
[Pointing to his Father's]
Walk this way.
[To the **AUDIENCE**]
Fare you well, and grant us your applause.

FOOTNOTES

[Footnote 1: From λαγχάνω, "to obtain by lot" or "heirship."]

[Footnote 2: From φαιδρός, "cheerful."]

[Footnote 3: From χαίρων, "rejoicing."]

[Footnote 4: From ἀντί, "opposite to," and φῶς, "light," or φῆμι, "to speak."]

[Footnote 5: From χρεμίζω, "to neigh;" delighting in horses.]

[Footnote 6: From θρασός, "boldness."]

[Footnote 7: From γναθός, "the jawbone;" a glutton.]

[Footnote 8: From παρά, "by," and μένω, "to remain."]

[Footnote 9: From Sangia in Phrygia, his native country.]

[Footnote 10: From δόναξ, "a reed."]

[Footnote 11: From σιμός, "flat-nosed."]

[Footnote 12: From Syria, his country; or from συρίσκος, "a basket of figs."]

[Footnote 13: From θεάομαι, "to look at."]

[Footnote 14: From πυθομένη, "asking questions."]

[Footnote 15: From Doris, their country, a part of Caria.]

[Footnote 16: From σώφρων, "prudent."]

[Footnote 17: From πᾶν, "all," and φιλός, "a friend."]

[Footnote 18: The Title]—Colman has the following remark on this Play: "This seems to have been the most popular of all the Comedies of Terence. Suetonius and Donatus both inform us that it was acted with the greatest applause, and that the Poet received a larger price for it from the Ædiles than had ever been paid for any before, namely, 8000 sesterces, which is about equal to 200 crowns, which in those times was a considerable sum."]

[Footnote 19: Acted twice]—This probably means "twice in one day." As it is generally supposed that something is wanting after the figures II, this is presumed to be "die," "in one day," in confirmation of which Suetonius informs us that it really was performed twice in one day. Donatus says it was performed three times, by which he may probably mean, twice on one day and once on another.]

[Footnote 20: Being Consuls]—M. Valerius Messala and C. Fannius Strabo were Consuls in the year from the building of the City 591, or B.C. 162.]

[Footnote 21: If there is one who thinks]—Ver. 4. He alludes to his old enemy, Luscus Lavinius, the Comic Poet, who is alluded to in the

Prologue to the Andria, and has since continued his attacks upon him.]

[Footnote 22: By translating literally]—Ver. 7. "Bene vertendo, at eosdem scribendo male." This passage has greatly puzzled some of the Commentators. Bentley has, however, it appears, come to the most reasonable conclusion; who supposes that Terence means by "bene vertere," a literal translation, word for word, from the Greek, by which a servile adherence to the idiom of that language was preserved to the neglect of the Latin idiom; in consequence of which the Plays of Luscus Lavinius were, as he remarks, "male scriptæ," written in bad Latin.]

[Footnote 23: Has published the Phasma]—Ver. 9. The "Φασμά," or "Apparition," was a play of Menander, so called, in which a young man looking through a hole in the wall between his father's house and that next door, sees a young woman of marvelous beauty, and is struck with awe at the sight, as though by an apparition; in the Play, the girl's mother is represented as having made this hole in the wall, and having decked it with garlands and branches that it may resemble a consecrated place; where she daily performs her devotions in company with her daughter, who has been privately brought up, and whose existence is unknown to the neighbors. On the youth coming by degrees to the knowledge that the object of his admiration is but a mortal, his passion becomes so violent that it will admit of no cure but marriage, with the celebration of which the Play concludes. Bentley gives us the above information from an ancient Scholiast, whose name is unknown, unless it is Donatus himself, which is doubtful. It would appear that Luscus Lavinius had lately made a translation of this Play, which, from its servile adherence to the language of the original, had been couched in ungrammatical language, and probably not approved of by the Audience. Donatus thinks that this is the meaning of the passage, and that, content with this slight reference to a well-known fact, the author passes it by in contemptuous silence.]

[Footnote 24: And in the Thesaurus has described]—Ver. 10. Cook has the following appropriate remark upon this passage: "In the 'Thesaurus,' or 'Treasure' of Luscus Lavinius, a young fellow, having wasted his estate by his extravagance, sends a servant to search his father's monument: but he had before sold the ground on which the monument was, to a covetous old man; to whom the servant applies to help him open the monument; in which they discover a hoard and a letter. The old fellow sees the treasure and keeps it; the young one goes to law with him, and the old man is represented as opening his cause first before the judge, which he begins with these words:—

'Athenienses, bellum cum Rhodiensibus,
Quod fuerit, quid ego prædicem?'

'Athenians, why should I relate the war with the Rhodians?' And he goes on in a manner contrary to the rules of court; which Terence objects to, because the young man, who was the plaintiff, should open his cause first. Thus far Bentley, from the same Scholiast [as referred to in the last Note]. This Note is a clear explanation of the four verses to which it belongs. Hare concurs with Madame Dacier in her opinion 'de Thesauro,' that it is only a part of the Phasma of Menander, and not a distinct Play; but were I not determined by the more learned Bentley, the text itself would not permit me to be of their opinion; for the words 'atque in Thesauro scripsit' seem plainly to me to be a transition to another Play. The subject of the Thesaurus is related by Eugraphius, though not with all the circumstances mentioned in my Note from Bentley." Colman also remarks here; "Menander and his contemporary Philemon, each of them wrote a Comedy under this title. We have in the above Note the story of Menander's; and we know that of Philemon's from the 'Trinummus' of Plautus, which was a Translation of it."]

[Footnote 25: Opportunity of viewing it]—Ver. 21. Colman thinks that this means something "stronger than merely being present at the representation," and he takes the meaning to be, that having obtained leave to peruse the MS., he furnished himself with objections against the piece, which he threw out when it came to be represented before the magistrates. Cooke thinks that the passage only means, "that he bustled and took pains to be near enough at the representation to see and hear plainly." The truth seems to be that Lavinius managed to obtain admission at the rehearsal or trial of the merits of the piece before the magistrates, and that he then behaved himself in the unseemly manner mentioned in the text.]

[Footnote 26: Produced the piece, but still had not deceived him]—Ver. 24. There is a pun here upon the resemblance in meaning of the words "verba dare" and "fabulam dare." The first expression means to "deceive" or "impose upon;" the latter phrase has also the same meaning, but it may signify as well "to represent" or "produce a Play." Thus the exclamation in its ambiguity may mean, "he has produced a Play, and has not succeeded in deceiving us," or "he has deceived us, and yet has not deceived us." This is the interpretation which Donatus puts upon the passage.]

[Footnote 27: Colax, an old Play of Plautus]—Ver. 25. Although Nonius Marcellus professes to quote from the Colax of Plautus (so called from the Greek Κολαξ, "a flatterer" or "parasite"), some scholars have disbelieved in the existence of any Play of Plautus known by that name. Cooke says: "If Plautus had wrote a Play under the title of 'Colax,' I should think it very unlikely that it should have escaped Terence's eye, considering how soon he flourished after Plautus, his being engaged in the same studies, and his having such opportunities to consult the libraries of the great; for though all learning was then confined to Manuscripts, Terence could have no difficulty in coming at the best copies. The character of the 'Miles Gloriosus' [Braggart Captain] here mentioned, I am inclined to think the same with that which is the hero of Plautus's Comedy, now extant, and called 'Miles Gloriosus,' from which Terence could not take his Thraso. Pyrgopolinices and Thraso are both full of themselves, both boast of their valor and their intimacy with princes, and both fancy themselves beloved by all the women who see them; and they are both played off by their Parasites, but they differ in their manner and their speech: Plautus's Pyrgopolinices is always in the clouds, and talking big, and of blood and wounds—Terence's Thraso never says too little nor much, but is an easy ridiculous character, continually supplying the Audience with mirth without the wild extravagant bluster of Pyrgopolinices; Plautus and Terence both took their soldiers and Parasites from Menander, but gave them different dresses." Upon this Note Colman remarks: "Though there is much good criticism in the above Note, it is certain that Plautus did not take his 'Miles Gloriosus' from the Colax of Menander, as he himself informs us it was translated from a Greek play called Ἀλάζων, 'the Boaster,' and the Parasite is but a trifling character in that play, never appearing after the first Scene."]

[Footnote 28: Hurrying servants]—Ver. 35. On the "currentes servi," see the Prologue to the Heautontimorumenos, l. 31. Ovid, in the Amores, B. i., El. 15, l. 17, 18, mentions a very similar combination of the characters of Menander's Comedy: "So long as the deceitful slave, the harsh father, the roguish procuress, and the cozening courtesan shall endure, Menander will exist."]

[Footnote 29: What, then, shall I do?]—Ver. 46. Phædria, on being sent for by Thais, breaks out into those words as he enters, after having deliberated upon his parting with her. Both Horace and Persius have imitated this passage in their Satires.]

[Footnote 30: What! I to her?]—Ver. 65. Donatus remarks that this is an abrupt manner of speaking familiarly to persons in anger; and that the sentences are thus to be understood, "I, go to her? Her, who has received him! Who has excluded me!"—inasmuch as indignation loves to deal in Ellipsis and Aposiopesis.]

[Footnote 31: The downfall of our fortunes]—Ver. 79. Colman observes, "There is an extreme elegance in this passage in the original; and the figurative expression is beautifully employed." "Calamitas" was originally a word used in husbandry, which signified the destruction of growing corn; because, as Donatus says,

"Comminuit calamum et segetem;"—"it strikes down the blades and standing corn."]

[Footnote 32: Approach this fire]—Ver. 85. "Ignem" is generally supposed to be used figuratively here, and to mean "the flame of love." Eugraphius, however, would understand the expression literally, observing that courtesans usually had near their doors an altar sacred to Venus, on which they daily sacrificed.]

[Footnote 33: Of course it's because]—Ver. 89. It must be observed that these words, commencing with "Sane, quia vero," in the original, are said by Phædria not in answer to the words of Thais immediately preceding, but to her previous question, "Cur non recta introibas?" "Why didn't you come into the house at once?" and that they are spoken in bitter irony.]

[Footnote 34: From Sunium]—Ver. 115. This was a town situate near a lofty Promontory of that name in Attica. It was famous for a fair which was held there. "Sunium's rocky brow" is mentioned by Byron in the song of the Greek Captive in the third Canto of Don Juan.]

[Footnote 35: Set out for Caria]—Ver. 126. This was a country of Asia Minor upon the sea-coast, opposite to the island of Rhodes.]

[Footnote 36: Servant-maid from Æthiopia]—Ver. 165. No doubt Æthiopian or negro slaves were much prized by the great, and those courtesans whose object it was to ape their manners.]

[Footnote 37: Ladies of quality]—Ver. 168. "Reginæ," literally "queens," here means women of rank and distinction.]

[Footnote 38: Paid twenty minæ]—Ver. 169. The "minæ" contained one hundred "drachmæ" of about 9¾d. each.]

[Footnote 39: Ah wretched me!]—Ver. 197. Donatus remarks that the Poet judiciously reserves that part of the plot to be told here, which Thais did not relate to Phædria in the presence of Parmeno; whom the Poet keeps in ignorance as to the rank of the damsel, that he may with the more probability dare to assist Chærea in his attempt on her.]

[Footnote 40: From the dispositions of other women]—Ver. 198. Donatus observes that this is one of the peculiar points of excellence shown by Terence, introducing common characters in a new manner, without departing from custom or nature; since he draws a good Courtesan, and yet engages the attention of the Spectators and amuses them. Colman has the following Note here: "Under the name of Thais, Menander is supposed to have drawn the character of his own mistress, Glycerium, and it seems he introduced a Courtesan of the same name into several of his Comedies. One Comedy was entitled 'Thais,' from which St. Paul took the sentence in his Epistle to the Corinthians, 'Evil communications corrupt good manners.'" Plutarch has preserved four lines of the Prologue to that Comedy, in which the Poet, in a kind of mock-heroic manner, invokes the Muse to teach him to depict the character of his heroine.]

[Footnote 41: Not any one was there]—Ver. 226-7. Very nearly the same words as these occur in the Mostellaria of Plautus, l. 29, 30: "Than whom, hitherto, no one of the youth of all Attica has been considered more temperate or equally frugal."]

[Footnote 42: Nor submit to blows]—Ver. 244. It has been remarked in the Notes to the Translation of Plautus that the Parasites had, in consequence of their state of dependence, to endure blows and indignities from their fellow-guests. Their attempts to be "ridiculi" or "drolls" were made in order to give some small return to their entertainers. See especially the character of Gelasimus in the Stichus of Plautus, and the words of Ergasilus in the Captivi, l. 88, 90. Diderot, as quoted by Colman, observes: "This is the only Scene in

Terence which I remember that can be charged with being superfluous. Thraso has made a present to Thais of a young girl. Gnatho is to convey her. Going along with her, he amuses himself with giving the Spectators a most agreeable eulogium on his profession. But was that the time for it? Let Gnatho pay due attention on the stage to the young woman whom he is charged with, and let him say what he will to himself, I consent to it."]

[Footnote 43: Fishmongers]—Ver. 257. "Cetarii;" strictly speaking, "dealers in large fish."]

[Footnote 44: Cooks]—Ver. 257. The "coqui" were in the habit of standing in the market-place for hire by those who required their services. See the Pseudolus, the Aulularia, and the Mercator of Plautus, and the Notes to Bohn's Translation. See also a remark on the knavish character of the sausage-makers in the Truculentus of Plautus, l. 110]

[Footnote 45: Become my follower]—Ver. 262. "Sectari." In allusion to the manners of the ancient Philosophers, who were wont to be followed by a crowd of their disciples, who were styled "sectatores" and "sectæ." Gnatho intends to found a new school of Parasites, who shall be called the "Gnathonics," and who, by their artful adulation, shall contrive to be caressed instead of being maltreated. Artotrogus, the Parasite in the Miles Gloriosus of Plautus, seems, however, to have forestalled Gnatho as the founder of this new school.]

[Footnote 46: I'm standing]—Ver. 271. "Quid agitur?" "Statur." The same joke occurs in the Pseudolus of Plautus, l. 457. "Quid agitur? Statur hic ad hunc modum?" "What is going on?" or "What are you about?" "About standing here in this fashion;" assuming an attitude. Colman observes that there is much the same kind of conceit in the "Merry Wives of Windsor."

FALSTAFF. "My honest lads, I will tell you what I am about." PISTOL. "Two yards or more."

Cooke has the following note: "'Quid agitur' is to be supposed to have a single meaning as spoken by Gnatho, but Parmeno archly renders it ambiguous by his answer. Our two first English translations, that by Bernard and that by Hoole, make nothing of it, nor indeed any other part of their author. Echard follows Madame Dacier, and perceives a joke; but he does not render 'quid, agitur' as the question ought to be translated. 'Quid agitur' sometimes means, 'What are you doing?' Sometimes, 'How do you do?' 'How are you?' or 'How goes the world with you?'"]

[Footnote 47: From the Piraeus]—Ver. 290. The Piraeus was the chief harbor of Athens, at the mouth of the Cephisus, about three miles from the City. It was joined to the town by two walls, one of which was built by Themistocles, and the other by Pericles. It was the duty of the Athenian youth to watch here in turn by way of precaution against surprise by pirates or the enemy.]

[Footnote 48: In your little room]—Ver. 310. Though "cellulam" seems to be considered by some to mean "cupboard" or "larder," it is more probable that it here signifies the little room which was appropriated to each slave in the family for his own use.]

[Footnote 49: Shoulders kept down and chests well girthed]—Ver. 314. Ovid, in the Art of Love, B. iii., l. 274, alludes to the "strophium" or "girth" here referred to: "For high shoulders, small pads are suitable; and let the girth encircle the bosom that is too prominent." Becker thinks that the "strophium" was different from the "fascia" or "stomacher," mentioned in the Remedy of Love, l. 338: "Does a swelling bosom cover all her breast, let no stomacher conceal it." From Martial we learn that the "strophium" was made of leather.]

[Footnote 50: Training for a boxer]—Ver. 315. "Pugilem." This means "robust as a boxer," or "athlete." These persons were naturally considered as the types of robustness, being dieted for the purpose of increasing their flesh and muscle.]

[Footnote 51: Complexion genuine]—Ver. 318. "Color verns." The same expression is used by Ovid, in the Art of Love, B. iii., l. 164: "Et melior vero quæritur arte color:" "And by art a color is sought superior to the genuine one."]

[Footnote 52: Full of juiciness]—Ver. 318. "Succi plenum." A similar expression occurs in the Miles Gloriosus of Plautus, l. 787, where Periplecomenus wishes inquiry to be made for a woman who is "siccam, at sucedam," "sober, but full of juice:" i.e. replete with the plumpness and activity of youth.]

[Footnote 53: The very flower of youth]—Ver. 319. Ovid makes mention of the "flos" or "bloom" of youth, Art of Love, B. ii., l. 663: "And don't you inquire what year she is now passing, nor under what Consulship she was born; a privilege which the rigid Censor possesses. And this, especially, if she has passed the bloom of youth, and her best years are fled, and she now pulls out the whitening hairs."]

[Footnote 54: Be my advocate]—Ver. 340. "Advocatus." It must be remembered that this word did not among the Romans bear the same sense as the word "advocate" does with us. The "advocati" were the friends of a man who accompanied him when his cause was pleaded, and often performed the part of witnesses; those who assisted a person in a dispute or difficulty were also his "advocati," and in this respect distantly resembled the "second" or "friend" of a party in the modern duel. In the Phormio, Hegio, Cratinus, and Crito are introduced as the "advocati" of Demipho. See also the Pænulus of Plautus, and the Notes to that Play in Bohn's Translation.]

[Footnote 55: An hour elapsed]—Ver. 341. "Hora" is here used to signify the long time, that, in his impatience, it appeared to him to be.]

[Footnote 56: It's all over with you,—you've said your last]—Ver. 347. "Ilicet" and "conclamatnm est," are words of mournful import, which were used with regard to the funeral rites of the Romans. "Ilicet," "you may begone," was said aloud when the funeral was concluded. "Conclamare," implied the ceremony of calling upon the dead person by name, before light was act to the funeral pile; on no answer being given, he was concluded to be really dead, and the pile was set fire to amid the cries of those present: "conclamatum est" would consequently signify that all hope has gone.]

[Footnote 57: Thais the Courtesan]—Ver. 352. Cooke remarks here, somewhat hypercritically as it would seem: "Thais is not called 'meretrix' here opprobriously, but to distinguish her from other ladies of the same name, who were not of the same profession."]

[Footnote 58: A Eunuch]—Ver. 356. Eunuchs formed part of the establishment of wealthy persons, who, in imitation of the Eastern nobles, confided the charge of their wives, daughters, or mistresses to them. Though Thais would have no such necessity for his services, her wish to imitate the "reginæ," or "great ladies," would make him a not unacceptable present. See the Addresses of Ovid to the Eunuch Bagoüs in the Amours, B. ii., El. 2, 3.]

[Footnote 59: as she is reported to be]—Ver. 361. Donatus remarks this as an instance of the art of Terence, in preserving the probability of Chærea's being received for the Eunuch. He shows hereby that he is so entirely a stranger to the family that he does not even know the person of Thais. It is also added that she has not been long in the neighborhood, and he has been on duty at the Piraeus. The meaning of his regret is, that, not knowing Thais, he will not have an opportunity of seeing the girl.]

[Footnote 60: Have to pay the penalty]—Ver. 381. "In me cadetur faba," literally, "the bean will be struck" or "laid about me;" meaning, "I shall have to smart for it." There is considerable doubt what is the origin of this expression, and this doubt existed as early as the time of Donatus. He says that it was a proverb either taken from the threshing of beans with a flail by the countrymen; or else from the circumstance of the cooks who have dressed the beans, but have not moistened them sufficiently, being sure to have them thrown at their heads, as though for the purpose of softening them. Neither of these solutions seems so probable as that suggested by Madame Dacier, that dried beans were inserted in the thongs of the "scuticæ," or "whips," with which the slaves were beaten. According to others the knots in the whips were only called "fabæ," from their resemblance to beans.]

[Footnote 61: Is it disgraceful]—Ver. 382. Donatus remarks that here Terence obliquely defends the subject of the Play.]

[Footnote 62: The most mighty King]—Ver. 397. It has been suggested that Darius III. is here alluded to, who was a contemporary of Menander. As however Pyrrhus, king of Epirus, is mentioned in this Play, there is no necessity to go out of the way to make Terence guilty of an anachronism. Madame Dacier suggests that Seleucus, king of part of Asia Minor, is meant; and as Thraso is called "a stranger" or "foreigner" toward the end of the Play, he probably was intended to be represented as a native of Asia and a subject of Seleucus. One of the Seleuci was also favored with the services of Pyrgopolinices, the "Braggart Captain" of Plantus, in the Miles Gloriosus. See l. 75 in that Play: "For King Seleucus entreated me with most earnest suit that I would raise and enlist recruits for him."]

[Footnote 63: You've just hit it]—Ver. 401. Colman here remarks, quoting the following passage from Shakspeare's "Love's Labor Lost," "That that Poet was familiarly acquainted with this Comedy is evident from the passage, 'Holofernes says, Novi hominem tanquam te. His humor is lofty, his discourse peremptory, his tongue filed, his eye ambitious, his gait majestical, and his general behavior vain, ridiculous, and Thrasonical.'" We may remark that the previous words of Gnatho, though spoken with reference to the King, contain a reproach against the Captain's boastfulness, though his vanity will not let him perceive it.]

[Footnote 64: In his eye]—Ver. 401. "In oculis" is generally supposed to mean "as dearly in his eyes." As, however, the Satraps of the East were called "the king's eyes," those who suppose that Darius is alluded to, might with some ground consider the passage as meaning that the king ranked him in the number of his nobles. See the Pænulus of Plautus, l. 693, and the Note in Bohn's Translation.]

[Footnote 65: You understand]—Ver. 405. He says this at the very moment when he is at a loss what to say next; the Parasite obligingly steps in to help him out with the difficulty.]

[Footnote 66: Indeed, of none]—Ver. 410. "Immo, nullorum arbitror, si tecum vivit." This expression which is used "aside," has two meanings, neither of which is complimentary to the Captain. It may mean, "he has no society if he associates with you," making the Captain equivalent to nobody; or it may signify, "if he associates with you he'll be sure to drive all his other acquaintances away."]

[Footnote 67: Over the Indian elephants]—Ver. 413. Here he shows his lofty position to perfection; he dares to take down the pride of one who commanded even the royal elephants. The Braggart Captain of Plautus comes into collision with the elephants themselves: l. 26. Artotrogus says to him, "In what a fashion it was you broke the fore-leg of even an elephant in India with your fist!"]

[Footnote 68: Looking out for game?]—Ver. 426. "Pulmentum," more strictly speaking, "A nice bit." Patrick has the following Note on this passage: "'Lepus tute es, et pulmentum quæris?' A proverbial expression in use at that time: the proper meaning of it, stripped of its figure, is, 'You are little more than a woman yourself, and do you want a mistress?'" We learn from Donatus and Vopiscus, that Livius Andronicus had used this proverb in his Plays before

Terence. Commentators who enter into a minute explanation of it offer many conjectures rather curious than solid, and of a nature not fit to be mentioned here. Donatus seems to think that allusion is made to a story prevalent among the ancient naturalists that the hare was in the habit of changing its sex.]

[Footnote 69: If, indeed, she loved me]—Ver. 446. Colman has the following Note upon this passage: "I am at a loss to determine whether it was in order to show the absurdity of the Captain or from inadvertence in the Poet, that Terence here makes Thraso and Gnatho speak in contradiction to the idea of Thais's wonderful veneration for Thraso, with which they opened the Scene."]

[Footnote 70: In exercises]—Ver. 477. Reference will be found made to the "palæstræ," or "places of exercise," in the Notes to the Translation of Plautus.]

[Footnote 71: If occasion served]—Ver. 479. The Aposiopesis in this line is very aptly introduced, on account of the presence of the female; but it admirably illustrates the abominable turpitude of the speaker, and perhaps in a somewhat more decent manner than that in which Plautus attributes a similar tendency to his Braggart Captain, l. 1111.]

[Footnote 72: Out of the very flames]—Ver. 491. This was a proverb expressive of the lowest degree of meanness and infamy. When they burned the bodies of the dead, it was the custom of the ancients to throw meat and various articles of food upon the funeral pile, and it was considered the greatest possible affront to tell a person that he was capable of snatching these things out of the flames.]

[Footnote 73: If Chremes should happen to come]—Ver. 513. This is the first allusion to the arrangement which ultimately causes the quarrel between Thais and the Captain.]

[Footnote 74: Had been offering a sacrifice]—Ver. 513. It was the custom to sacrifice before entering on affairs of importance. Thus, too, Jupiter, in the Amphitryon of Plautus, l. 938, speaks of offering sacrifice on his safe return.]

[Footnote 75: Our rings were given]—Ver. 541. It was the custom of parties who agreed to join in a "symbola," or "club" or "picnic" entertainment, to give their rings as pledges to the "rex convivii," or "getter up the feast." Stakes were also deposited on making bets at races. See Ovid's Art of Love, B. i., l. 168.]

[Footnote 76: To meet my death]—Ver. 550. There is a passage in the Othello of Shakspeare extremely similar to this:
—"If I were now to die,
I were now to be most happy; for, I fear,
My soul hath her content so absolute,
That not another comfort, like to this,
Succeeds in unknown fate."]

[Footnote 77: In the inner apartments]—Ver. 579. The "Gynecæa," or women's apartments, among the Greeks, always occupied the interior part of the house, which was most distant from the street, and there they were kept in great seclusion.]

[Footnote 78: A few novices of girls]—Ver. 582. These "noviciæ" were young slaves recently bought, and intended to be trained to the calling of a Courtesan.]

[Footnote 79: At a certain painting]—Ver. 584. See the story of Jupiter and Danaë, the daughter of Acrisius, king of Argos, in the Metamorphoses of Ovid, B. iv., l. 610. Pictures of Venus and Adonis, and of Jupiter and Ganymede, are mentioned in the Menæchmi of Plautus; l. 144, and paintings on the walls are also mentioned in the Mostellaria of Plantus, l. 821, where Tranio tries to impose upon Theuropides by pretending to point out a picture of a crow between two vultures.]

[Footnote 80: How Jove]—Ver. 584. Donatus remarks here that this was "a very proper piece of furniture for the house of a Courtesan, giving an example of loose and mercenary love, calculated to excite wanton thoughts, and at the same time hinting to the young lover that he must make his way to the bosom of his mistress, like Jupiter to Danaë, in a shower of gold. Oh the avarice of harlots!"]

[Footnote 81: A poor creature of a mortal]—Ver. 591. "Homuncio." He uses this word the better to contrast his abject nature as a poor mortal with the majesty of Jupiter. St. Augustin refers to this passage. The preceding line is said by Donatus to be a parody on a passage by Ennius.]

[Footnote 82: Take this fan]—Ver. 595. As to the fans of the ancients, see the Trinummus of Plautus, l. 252, and the Note to the passage in Bohn's Translation. See also the Amours of Ovid, B. iii., El. 2, l. 38.]

[Footnote 83: Chattered aloud]—Ver. 600. This line bears a strong resemblance to two lines found in Anstey's new Bath Guide:

"And how the young ladies all set up their clacks,   All the while an old woman was rubbing their backs."]

[Footnote 84: I slily looked askance]—Ver. 601. This way of looking aside, "limis," is mentioned in the Miles Gloriosus of Plautus, where Milphidippa tells Acroteleutium to look at the Captain sideways, "Aspicito limis," l. 1217; also in the Bacchides, l. 1131. Those familiar with the works of Hogarth will readily call to mind the picture of Bedlam in the Rake's Progress, whore the young woman is looking askance through her fan at the madman in his cell.]

[Footnote 85: Through the fan]—Ver. 602. This shows that the fan was probably one made of thin boards, and not of feathers.]

[Footnote 86: *So short-lived*]—Ver. 605. Colman has the following Note here: "Short indeed, considering the number of incidents, which, according to Chærea's relation, are crowded into it. All the time allowed for this adventure is the short space between the departure of Thais and Thraso and the entrance of Chærea; so that all this variety of business of sleeping, bathing, ravishing, &c., is dispatched during the two soliloquies of Antipho and Chærea, and the short Scene between Chremes and Pythias. The truth is, that a very close adherence to the unities often drives the Poet into as great absurdities as the perfect violation of them."]

[Footnote 87: *Took off her golden jewels*]—Ver. 627. This was probably because it was contrary to the laws of Athens for a Courtesan to appear with gold or jewels in the street. Madame Dacier suggests another reason, in which there is some force, although it is ridiculed by Cooke. Thais may have supposed that the Captain, when irritated, might not have scrupled to take them away from her. Indeed, nothing would be more probable, than that he would be ready to take them by way of security for the return of the slave, whom he had thus, to no purpose, presented to her. In reference to the preceding line, we may remark that it was not customary among the Greeks for females of good character to appear at table with strangers.]

[Footnote 88: *While I was going*]—Ver. 629. Donatus remarks that here the Poet artfully finds a reason to bring Phædria back again; as he at first with equal art sent him out of the way, to give probability to those incidents necessary to happen in his absence.]

[Footnote 89: *At a distance*]—Ver. 640. "Extremâ lineâ." There have been many suggestions offered for the origin of this figurative expression. Some suggest that it alludes to the last or lowest stage of the supposed ladder of love; others that it refers to the first or elementary line traced by the student, when beginning to learn the art of painting. It is however more generally thought to be a metaphor taken from the chariot-races in the Circus, where, in going round the turning-place, he who was nearest was said "currere in primâ lineâ;" the next, "in secundâ;" and so on to the last, who took the widest range, and was said to run "in extremâ lineâ."]

[Footnote 90: In party-colored clothes]—Ver. 683. It was the custom to dress Eunuchs in party-colored clothes of bright hue. Most probably it was from them that the "motley" descended to the fools and buffoons of the Middle Ages.]

[Footnote 91: With a speckled complexion]—Ver. 689. "Colore stellionino;" probably having spots or freckles on his face like a "stellio" or "lizard."]

[Footnote 92: Have done a service to her]—Ver. 722. Though some would have "illi" here to refer to the damsel, and others again to Phædria, it is pretty clear that Madame Dacier is right in suggesting that Thais is the person meant.]

[Footnote 93: Casket with the tokens]—Ver. 752. It was the custom with the ancients when they exposed their children, to leave with them some pledge or token of value, that they might afterward be recognized by means of them. The catastrophes of the Curculio, the Rudens, and other Plays of Plautus, are brought about by taking advantage of this circumstance. The reasons for using these tokens will be stated in a future Note.]

[Footnote 94: Is a foreigner]—Ver. 758. And therefore the more unlikely to obtain redress from an Athenian tribunal. See the Andria, l. 811, and the Note to the passage.]

[Footnote 95: And his maniple]—Ver. 775. We learn from the Fasti of Ovid, B. iii., l. 117-8, that in early times the Roman armies carried bundles or wisps of hay upon poles by way of standards. "A long pole used to bear the elevated wisps, from which circumstance the manipular soldier derives his name." It appears from this passage, and from other authors, that to every troop of one hundred men a "manipulus" or wisp of hay (so called from "manum implere," to "fill the hand," as being "a handful"), was assigned as a standard, and hence in time the company itself obtained the name of "manipulus," and the soldier, a member of it, was called "manipularis." The "centurio," or "leader of a hundred," was the commanding officer of the "manipulus."]

[Footnote 96: With a dish-clout]—Ver. 776. "Peniculo." This word meant a sponge fastened to a stick, or the tail of a fox or an ox, which was used as dusters or dish-clouts are at the present day for cleaning tables, dishes, or even shoes. See the Menæchmi of Plautus, ver. 77 and 391.]

[Footnote 97: Be behind the second rank]—Ver. 780. "Post principia." The Captain, with that discretion which is the better part of valor, chooses the safest place in his army. The "principes" originally fought in the van, fronting the enemy, and behind them were the "hastati" and the "triarii." In later times the "hastati" faced the enemy, and the "principes" were placed in the middle, between them and the "triarii;" but though no longer occupying the front place, they still retained the name. Thraso, then, places himself behind the middle line.]

[Footnote 98: Pyrrhus used to proceed]—Ver. 782. He attempts to defend his cowardice by the example of Pyrrhus, the powerful antagonist of the Romans, and one of the greatest generals of antiquity. He might have more correctly cited the example of Xerxes, who, according to Justin, did occupy that position in his army.]

[Footnote 99: I could very much]—Ver. 785. Although Vollbehr gives these words to Gnatho, yet, judging from the context, and the words "ex occulto," and remembering that Thais and Chremes are up at the window, there is the greatest probability that these are really the words of Thais addressed aside to Chremes.]

[Footnote 100: You gallows-bird]—Ver. 797. "Furcifer;" literally, "bearer of the furca."]

[Footnote 101: As befits gallant soldiers]—Ver. 814. Beaumont and Fletcher not improbably had this scene in view in their picture of the mob regiment in Philaster. The ragged regiment which Shakspeare places under the command of Falstaff was not very unlike it, nor that which owned the valiant Bombastes Furioso as its Captain.]

[Footnote 102: At Antipho's]—Ver. 839. Madame Dacier here observes that Chærea assigns very natural reasons for not having changed his dress; in which the art of Terence is evident, since the sequel of the Play makes it absolutely necessary that Chærea should appear again before Thais in the habit which he wore while in the house.]

[Footnote 103: Pick daintily about]—Ver. 935. He seems here to reprehend the same practice against which Ovid warns his fair readers, in his Art of Love, B. iii. l. 75. He says, "Do not first take food at home," when about to go to an entertainment. Westerhovius seems to think that "ligurio" means, not to "pick daintily," but "to be fond of good eating;" and refers to the Bacchides of Plautus as portraying courtesans of the "ligurient" kind, and finds another specimen in Bacchis in the Heautontimorumenos.]

[Footnote 104: This advantage]—Ver. 970. Donatus here observes that the Poet introduces Laches, as he has Parmeno just before, in a state of perfect tranquillity, that their sudden change of feeling may be the more diverting to the Audience.]

[Footnote 105: For some occasion]—Ver. 999. We learn from Donatus that Menander was more explicit concerning the resentment of Laches against Thais, on account of her having corrupted Phædria.]

[Footnote 106: As I knew]—Ver. 1003. She enjoyed it the more, knowing that the old man had nothing to fear, as he had just heard the fiction which she had imparted to Parmeno. Donatus observes that the terror of Laches accounts for his sudden consent to the union of Chærea with Pamphila; for though he could not settle the matter any other way with credit, he was glad to find that his son had made an unequal match rather than endangered his life. Colman, however, observes with considerable justice: "I think Chærea apologizes still better for this arrangement in the Scene with Thais at the opening of this Act, where he says that he is confident of obtaining his father's consent, provided Pamphila proves to be a citizen; and, indeed, the match between them is rather a reparation of an injury done to her than a degradation of himself."]

[Footnote 107: In return for that present of yours]—Ver. 1022. By the present she means Chærea in the disguise of the Eunuch.]

[Footnote 108: Through betrayal of myself]—Ver. 1023. Which betrays itself by its own squeaking.]

[Footnote 109: Hercules served Omphale]—Ver. 1026. He alludes to the story of Omphale, Queen of Lydia, and Hercules. Being violently in love with her, the hero laid aside his club and boar's skin, and in the habit of a woman plied the spindle and distaff with her maids. See a curious story of Omphale, Hercules, and Faunus, in the Fasti of Ovid, B. ii. l. 305. As to the reappearance of Thraso here, Colman has the following remarks: "Thraso, says Donatus, is brought back again in order to be admitted to some share in the good graces of Thais, that he may not be made unhappy at the end of the Play; but surely it is an essential part of the poetical justice of Comedy to expose coxcombs to ridicule and to punish them, though without any shocking severity, for their follies."]

[Footnote 110: With a slipper]—Ver. 1027. He doubtless alludes to the treatment of Hercules by Omphale; and, according to Lucian, there was a story that Omphale used to beat him with her slipper or sandal. On that article of dress, see the Notes to the Trinummus of Plautus, l. 252.]

[Footnote 111: To the patronage of my father]—Ver. 1038. It was the custom at Athens for strangers, such as Thais was, to put themselves under the protection (in clientelam) of some wealthy citizen, who, as their patron, was bound to protect them against injury. An exactly parallel case to the present is found in the Miles Gloriosus of Plautus, l. 799, where the wealthy Periplecomenus says, "Habeo, eccillam, meam clientam, meretricem adolescentulam." "Why, look, I have one, a dependent of mine, a courtesan, a very young woman."]

[Footnote 112: Been rolling that stone]—Ver. 1084. Donatus thinks that he alludes to the story of Sisyphus, who, in the Infernal Regions, was condemned eternally to roll a stone up a hill, which, on arriving at the summit, immediately fell to the bottom.]

[Footnote 113: Make him over to you]—Ver. 1086. "Vobis propino." The word "propino" was properly applied to the act of tasting a cup of wine, and then handing it to another; he means that he has had his taste of the Captain, and is now ready to hand him over to them.]

[Footnote 114: He quite deserves it]—Ver. 1087. Cooke has the following appropriate remark: "I can not think that this Play, excellent as it is in almost all other respects, concludes consistently with the manners of gentlemen; there is a meanness in Phædria and Chærea consenting to take Thraso into their society, with a view of fleecing him, which the Poet should have avoided."]

Henry Thomas Riley (Translator)

Riley was born in June 1816, the only son of Henry Riley of Southwark, an ironmonger.

He was educated at Chatham House, Ramsgate, and at Charterhouse School. University was at Trinity College, Cambridge, but at the end of his first term he moved to Clare College where he was admitted on 17th December 1834 and elected a scholar on 24th January 1835.

He graduated B.A. in 1840.

Riley was called to the bar at the Inner Temple on 23rd November 1847, but early in life he worked for booksellers, editing and translating. These skills were to bring him perhaps the real jewels of his legacy with his translations of Terence, Ovid, Plautus and Lucan during the 1850's.

When the Royal Charter of April 1869 set up the Historical Manuscripts Commission he was engaged as an inspector and tasked with examining the archives of various municipal corporations, the muniments of the colleges at Oxford and Cambridge, and the documents in the registries of various bishops and chapters.

Henry Thomas Riley died at Hainault House, the Crescent, Selhurst, Croydon, on 14th April 1878, aged 61.

Terence – A Concise Bibliography

Andria (The Girl from Andros) (166 BC)
Hecyra (The Mother-in-Law) (165 BC)
Heauton Timorumenos (The Self-Tormentor) (163 BC)
Phormio (The Scheming Parasite) (161 BC)
Eunuchus (The Eunuch) (161 BC)

Adelphoe (The Brothers) (160 BC)

The first known printed edition of Terence appeared in Strasbourg in 1470.

www.ingramcontent.com/pod-product-compliance
Lightning Source LLC
Chambersburg PA
CBHW022119040426
42450CB00006B/761

Eunuchus (The Eunuch) by Terence

A Translation by Henry Thomas Riley

Publius Terentius Afer is better known to us as the Roman playwright, Terence.

Much of his life, especially the early part, is either unknown or has conflicting sources and accounts.

His birth date is said to be either 185 BC or a decade earlier: 195 BC. His place of birth is variously listed as in, or, near Carthage, or, in Greek Italy to a woman taken to Carthage as a slave. It is suggested that he lived in the territory of the Libyan tribe that the Romans called Afri, near Carthage, before being brought to Rome as a slave. Probability suggests that it was there, in North Africa, several decades after the destruction of Carthage by the Romans in 146 BC, at the end of the Punic Wars, that Terence spent his early years.

One reliable fact is that he was sold to P. Terentius Lucanus, a Roman senator, who had him educated and, impressed by his literary talents, freed him.

These writing talents were to ensure his legacy as a playwright down through the millennia. His comedies, partially adapted from Greek plays of the late phases of Attic Comedy, were performed for the first time around 170–160 BC. All six of the plays he has known to have written have survived.

Indeed, thanks to his simple conversational Latin, which was both entertaining and direct, Terence's works were heavily used by monasteries and convents during the Middle Ages and The

Renaissance. Scribes often learned Latin through the copious copying of Terence's texts. Priests and nuns often learned to speak Latin through re-enactment of Terence's plays. Although his plays often dealt with pagan material, the quality and distinction of his language promoted the copying and preserving of his text by the church. This preservation enabled his work to influence a wide spectrum of later Western drama.

When he was 25 (or 35 depending on which year of birth you ascribe too), Terence travelled to Greece but never returned. It has long been assumed that he died at some point during the journey.

Of his own family nothing is known, except that he fathered a daughter and left a small but valuable estate just outside Rome.

His most famous quotation reads: "Homo sum, humani nihil a me alienum puto", or "I am human, and I think nothing human is alien to me."

Index of Contents
DRAMATIS PERSONÆ
SCENE:—Athens; before the houses of Laches and Thais.
THE SUBJECT
THE TITLE OF THE PLAY
EUNUCHUS; THE EUNUCH
THE SUMMARY OF C. SULPITIUS APOLLINARIS
THE PROLOGUE
ACT THE FIRST
SCENE I
SCENE II
SCENE III
ACT THE SECOND
SCENE I
SCENE II
SCENE III